I'm Fine

A BATHROOM BOOK FOR SENIORS

Angela

For Marc's Mom

That's me — + proud
of it!!

X Carter

I'm Fine

A BATHROOM BOOK FOR SENIORS

Susan Carter

With illustrations by
Susanne Ritchie & David Shkolny

I'M FINE
A Bathroom Book For Seniors

Copyright © Susan Carter, 2022

Published by Susan Carter, Leduc, Canada

ISBN:
Paperback	978-1-77354-432-8
ebook	978-1-77354-434-2

Publication assistance and digital printing in Canada by

PUBLISHING
PageMaster.ca

Thoughts

March 29, 2021

It's more than a year into this pandemic. I spent the first year thinking how great it was to get so many of my projects done. Now, not so much! I took a course for three months that I spent lots of time and effort on. It's been a month since I finished and I've spent that restlessly trying to buckle down to something else. The projects are still in the store room, but I think it's the attitude dip that's preventing me from getting something "done".

So... I decided to throw myself into finishing this book. I think the way the pandemic is going I have time.... Hopefully I'm being optimistic with that statement and I don't have time....

I promise to only write up-beat things about the pandemic and not start weeping about all the petty hardships my family has endured. Sure, life isn't back to "normal", but we are (at the time of this writing) all healthy. My Dad is ninety-two. He is in a great extended care facility. All his physical needs are met and we talk via Skype. My husband and I stay at home avoiding each other on separate floors of our condo. I do what I feel like doing downstairs and every once in a while, vacuum upstairs. He goes out while I'm still asleep to take advantage of senior hour shopping. He brings home boxed food to warm up to tell me supper is ready. We see our daughter, her husband and our seven-year-old twin grandsons once a week to have coffee outside. We keep our distance and wear a mask most of the time... all of us have enough money. We're fine.

I hope you are fine. I hope reading my stories can help when you're not fine.

I'm fine...

Or: Falling for a lovely man

December 15, 2016, I fell on ice in Waterville, Nova Scotia in front of the Fire Station... It was a dumb move, going outside, it WAS winter, there was snow on the ground, and unfortunately there was ice under the snow!

As I lay on this ice in agonizing pain chanting the three really juicy curse words I knew, I heard a truck drive up... Oh just run over me now and put me out of my misery I thought. Not to be, the lovely man stopped and asked various questions that have struck me funny in hindsight. Are you hurt? – no I'm just laying here on the road making snow angels! Can I help you? – Yes, if you can do time travel; let's go back in time so I don't do this stupid fall. What can I do to help? – PLEASE just run over me!

He did help by lifting me out of the snow angel position and getting me to my car. I told him (foolishly I now realize) that I could drive home. He thought I should go to the hospital – probably by the odd grey colour of my face. But no, I said I was "fine". After three days of unabated agonizing pain, I went to a doctor at the clinic who told me I was "lucky" because nothing was broken and I just had the pain. I saw the chiropractor. She assured me that my arm was fine and then twirled my arm and did other rude things to it. I'm thinking she did this to prove her point.

After six weeks of being "lucky" and the advice of my massage therapist and acupuncturist, I decided to gamble and go to the clinic again. Another doctor was skeptical, but reluctantly agreed to an X-ray – yes, my arm was broken, and in hindsight I should have been doing a sling thing and resting the arm instead of listening to "professionals" and one husband who said I should "use it or lose it"!

My arm continued to give me pain. I told a doctor I had "chronic pain" – OH no, it's not chronic. Well, what DO you call it when you've had constant pain for four months? Being a woman helps though. Women talk to each other about their pains (often childbirth, but that's another story...) Someone told me that going to see an Osteopath could help. OK, worth a try. I phoned all the Osteopaths in the Valley (in Nova Scotia; actually, called the Annapolis Valley). I took the first appointment I could get. My Osteopath was young... but very nice. She told me that if she couldn't help me in two or three sessions, I should see someone else. This was a new approach – most appointment people just want you to keep coming back. The first two appointments didn't help. On the third appointment, she asked if I would be all right to see someone else. OK. In came a wonderful older woman. She laid her hands on my shoulder for a few minutes. The pain went away faster than she did. WOW, a biblical experience I thought. What did she do? Well, apparently the mesh inside the bone needed to be re-aligned. WOW, the pain never came back.

It's been a long icy road to being able to use my arm, but I'm happy to say honestly this time that I'm "fine".

If I could, I would thank the lovely man who stopped to help me and explain to him that being a female in a vulnerable position prevented me from accepting help from a well-meaning stranger.

The moral of the story is to be cautious of icy roads and perhaps take a class on "how to fall without breaking anything" from a stunt person! Perhaps this class should be a requirement for getting your pension!

Susan Carter

'm dedicating this book to my dad, Vern Robinson. It's not because I walk, talk and think like him... it's because he taught me so many things.

He is ninety-three as I write this story. He is the perfect senior... he has always kept busy. He is always thinking of ways to fix something – whether that's our house or his room at the "home" (his reference - not mine). The last thing he was doing was putting Mactac on boxes because; well because... I never found out exactly what he was up to on that one.

He learned how to play the ukulele when he was eighty-three. Then he visited me in Nova Scotia to go to the Ukulele Ceilidh in Liverpool so we could attend all the fun together.

When he needed to get dentures, he decided to learn how to play the clarinet. He was worried that he might not be able to play the trombone with dentures. Then he could play yet another instrument. When a music show came on T.V. when I was growing up, he would sit down and chord along with all the songs on the piano. He played mouth organ as well. He was a whole act at one time!

Over the years, he always listened to whatever scheme I came up with. When I was in grade eight, I decided I wanted to do leather work. I got all the equipment I needed for Christmas and my birthday. When I was forty, both Mom and Dad listened as I told them I wanted to try stand-up. Dad has given me many joke ideas over the years... some I used, some not... yet.

So, I thought I would share one of his stories with you...

Woman Bites Husband to Death

(Based on an actual news story)

It seems that this forty-five-year-old woman was very "Horney" and wanted to have a bit of sex with her sixty-five-year-old husband. However, he was not in the same mood as she was at the time. She got very angry with him and attacked him and started to bite him all over his arms, all over his legs, and all over his abdomen. The man was putting up quite a struggle. In fact, he even phoned 911 and when he phoned, she was still biting him and when they played the tape back, he was screaming for all to hear.

I understand that the man may have been a bit under the weather. His body had a history of diabetes, heart trouble, and other circulatory problems. Now I also understand that if you are suffering from diabetes, heart trouble, and other circulatory problems, you may not want to have sex just whenever she wants to. Women of all people should understand this point of view. But I also don't think that he would have to pay for this with his life. Now I have heard of guys that may have given up their life because they wanted to have sex when the woman that they were near didn't want it, but that's different altogether.

After doing an autopsy, the forensic pathologist said that it was likely that the bites were to blame for the fact that he died. Also, the loss of blood was maybe a bit of a factor in the death.

Now the report did not say when she was doing this biting. I assume that it was before she had sex and not after she had sex and wanted some more. Now if it was after, I think I can understand the man a bit more.

There is another thought that enters my mind; will she be on "America's Most Wanted" T.V. show? I think that she might be because if she has that type of desire, then most American men will probably want her.

Another thought that I had was that if there will be a lot of "copy cat" activities such as this, I am sure none will ever take place in any of the accommodations that are devoted to seniors. The reasons that I have are that most of the seniors put their teeth in a glass before they go to bed and the only damage that they could do is probably "gnaw" their mates to death.

If such were the case, the mate may die of boredom while all that gnawing is going on!

Lately Dad isn't as good at listening to my ideas, mainly because he doesn't have his hearing aids in.

I walk, talk and think like Dad. Unfortunately, I look like him too!

Susan Carter

Saving Millions

December, 2008

Dear Editor,

I have been reflecting this Christmas season about what I can do to help people – what is the best way to use my time and energy to do the most good. I've been struck by the fact that Christmas truly is an all-year endeavor!

Last summer I feel I contributed to the flagging economy. Every little bit helps. I went into my local bank and withdrew $60.00 for a little bit of a spending spree (usually I withdraw $40.00). I was stunned to get 2 twenties and a hundred! I seriously thought I'd won money in a promotion and I went to the nearest teller to report my "winnings". I was then stunned to realize the "bank" had made a mistake! My hundred was quickly replaced with a twenty as the tellers speculated on how such an error had occurred. Months have passed and I did not get a phone call, a coffee card or even a thank you card; to help me over my $80.00 withdrawal withdrawal.

I realize that not only had I helped the bank by giving them the money back, I had NOT received the thank you card and stamp that would have seriously impacted the environment and would have put the bank into even more debt. Phone calls cost money and time, and hey, I've since quit drinking coffee! I know I have single handedly saved the banks in Canada millions!

Every little bit I can do during this Christmas season gives me a special glow, and what more can a person do than help bail out multi-million-dollar corporations!

Yours truly,

I did start drinking coffee again... I couldn't help myself!

Susan Carter

What makes YOU happy?

I was going through one of my mental lists the other day... I do a "gratitude" list in my head every once in a while, usually when my husband is complaining about politics. I do a "things to do" list, but since I've retired it is a short, lost, or slightly crumpled list. It occurred to me to make a "happiness" list.

Twin story: I was visiting my (at that time) very young twins. One of the activities they loved was to dance to various types of music that was selected by their mother. The Minions first movie was very popular and they danced to that music – Aaron watched and copied the dance moves; Braden just ran to the beat! One of their favourites was... "Happy" by Pharrell Williams and it became one of my favourites too. I just sang the background that repeated the word happy because I didn't catch all the other words!

So... what makes me happy? Lots of things make me happy. Good food that someone else has prepared, sleeping through the night, and of course Grandsons. But what gives me that ecstatic feeling, perhaps it's the same hormone rush those athletes get when they are in the zone, is singing. Singing very loudly to a song that has a great melody and a great beat makes me happy. It doesn't matter if I don't know the real words; I just make up new ones. The genre doesn't matter – I like some country twanging, I like yodelling, and I like some opera sung by Spike Jones.

I think I'll try singing along to some You Tube songs early in the morning; it might be better than coffee!

Eco Winter Wonderland

Tune: Winter Wonderland

Sleigh bells ring, are you listenin'?
Yes I am, the horse is glistenin'
I bought her to save gas
But she's a real pain in the ass
Clomping through a eco-wonderland

Gone away is the old car
Here to stay – she's no Jaguar
She's just an old nag
A regular fleabag
Clomping through a eco-wonderland

Through the meadow we will take a shortcut
Gosh I hope she really knows the way
Where the heck's the GPS? I need one
Looks like Trigger's leading me astray!

Later on, I'm a-digging
And a flask, I'm a-swigging

We're stuck in the snow
This nag has to go
This sure ain't no friggin wonderland!

*Another Bent/Carter parody. I've sung this song during the Christmas season... with good reviews!

Stand up Women's issues

Sent to CBC Radio Canada, May 26, 2015

I was saddened to hear of the sexual harassment of the three female comics interviewed on your show.

I too am a female comic. I decided to start doing Stand Up when I was 40. The perfect age for me; I was able to 'hide' my sexuality behind the middle age invisibility a lot of us experience after we turn 40.

Luckily the heckling I experience is generically JUST (and I emphasize JUST) anti-female, I'd experienced specific sexual harassment when I had large breasts; through my late teens and early twenties – when I was innocently walking on a sidewalk! It was NOT my best time; perhaps that is why I waited to start my stand-up career until I was forty – long after my breast reduction operation. I hung around Yuk Yuks in Edmonton with many eighteen-year-old boys who wanted to be the next "big thing". As a Junior High School teacher through the day, it was an interesting experience. I had a career and I'd started doing stand up as a stress outlet. Teaching at that time was going through a massive shift in Alberta and I personally needed something else to think about.

When I started charging money for my act, I specialized in "large groups of drunken women", so I didn't have a whole lot of trouble due to harassment. I did a grand total of two bars and was not thrilled with the experience. I ended up trading a lot of insults with the clients – I'm good at that because it's a lot like my day job teaching junior high. The bonus here is that I can say exactly what I think while on stage in a bar! I also had a secret weapon. I brought my husband to the gigs. He stayed in the audience and if the heckling went on too long, he would heckle the heckler... just enough so I could focus on my act and not the heckler. My husband is very quick witted and did the man-to-man competition very well, especially because HE wasn't drunk!

After I retired from full time Teaching, I decided to concentrate on working at Teachers Conventions. With thirty years of teaching experience, I had lots of audience specific jokes, and I'm very happy to be doing jokes in the morning. Without a drink in their hands, the audience isn't as likely to spew out sexual harassment, especially when their principal could be in the audience as well. Helping teachers teach humour to girls has become one of my passions.

Comedy is a very interesting business. As I studied the business, I realized that men can get away with so much more than women. When a guy is dirty, the men laugh because, well, not pretending to understand men, they understand each other! The women in the audience will laugh and say to themselves "aren't they cute"! Cute is on so many levels. When women are dirty the men are uncomfortable and the women say "tisk"! Double standards of course, but that's the way it is. I was able to do MANY ladies nights, lots of church shows and corporate events. I am happy doing stand up in my chosen genres, but there sure is a long way to total equality in the comedy business.

Yours truly,

Full Moon is not a good time to visit that Medical Quack

A letter to my Chiropractor

I know today was a full moon, I had a bad day too... but when I leave your office in tears, I feel you should discuss your relationships with your patients. I came to the office today to straighten up my back. I did not come to your office for the following:

- "It's been years since you've been here." Said by both the Doctor and the receptionist.
- You don't exercise enough
- I may refuse to treat you if you don't sweat. Your health should be high on your priority list
- When I needed to borrow five dollars from my husband to pay my bill, a comment was made... Mental health is also high on my priority list.
Guessing my age at forty did not impress me either

I was thirty-eight at the time! I never sweat – it's genetic. Dad, who is ninety-three at the time I'm writing this book, never sweats either.

*I lose my sense of humour during full moon

The Cat owns us....

I'm a little reluctant to report that my husband and I are now owned by a cat. It was insidious – we really don't know what happened. This cat was given to us by a friend whose neighbor was unable to take care of him. Our friend's cat was miss-named Fluff and would not put up with a rival. Ringo moved in and loudly protested the idea that he was now an indoor cat. He was adopted just before winter and he reluctantly agreed to stay inside; after all, the weather was ugly. Little did we know that he was sitting on his newly purchased perch looking out the window making plans for spring.

While he was sitting on his perch making plans, he was starting to wrap us around his very long, very sharp claws. As is the case with all manipulative children, he started small. Small enough that we really didn't know what was hitting us on the "upside of the head". He wanted one of us to stand by his food dish as he ate. We knew that he didn't need the food because there was food in his dish 24/7. It's now come to the place where one of us stands there telling him what a good boy he is as he takes furtive glances at us as he scarfs down his dry food. He doesn't want or need the food; we figure it's just a ploy for attention. The reason we figured this out is the amount of food that hits the floor as he sneaks glances at us. He now has three dishes of food. One dish upstairs in the Living room that Alan looks after and two downstairs. One is for the dry food and one for his once-a-day wet food.

The next step to ownership of Seniors is to distain the water dish. A water dish just isn't good enough for our Ringo. He tried the fresh water toilet route, but we found the strength to put a stop to that ploy by leaving the lids down. He one-upped that though. He waits for one of us to go to the bathroom and comes and sits. He's waiting for us to turn on the tub water and spread it around so he can get into the bathtub and lick up our epithelial skin cells along with the fresh water. He used to jump on the counter and wait for us to turn on the tap for him, but he's realized that he expends less energy and it's easier on his feet if he doesn't jump up and down from the counter. There is a lot more water in the bath tub to drink.

Ringo is a very vocal cat. He wore us down by the spring wanting to go outside. We finally allowed the outside thing. It was just so we could do more chores. Flea removal happened when we noticed that he was scratching. I purchased diatamatious earth to save the environment. He hates it. He punishes me for days after I've applied that stuff. Then there's corpse removal. Ringo was a great hunter in his former home. He took down a rabbit although he hasn't mentioned that in his memoirs. Then, of course, there's worm removal; the inevitable result of the corpses in the back yard. But after months of contract negotiations, Ringo realized that in order to go outside he had to learn to come when he was called. He also follows us around the neighborhood like a dog. When we visit the neighbors for a chit chat, he comes to hear what the gossip is. When we try to go for a walk he comes too. He has to be put in the house while we're gone.

After a few years of this uneasy truce, Ringo decided to up his game. He decided he NEEDED to be out all night. Yelling NO at him just kept the yowling quiet for a few minutes. Finally, my husband, who gets up lots to wander the house frequently at night, gave in and let him out.... Whenever Ringo demanded to go....

The upside was the fact that we didn't need to clean the litter box all summer. OOPS, we forgot, winter is back. We've been storm stayed for three days running. The cat needed to go Number 2. We knew it, he knew it and the howling was on. I could not believe it. On day 3 I was putting him in the litter box and telling him...

Good Boy as I watched him poop!

Where did we go wrong? Perhaps that's the wrong question, perhaps the question is... is this the inevitable result of being grandparents? Are we practicing for our grandchildren? Are we indulging a furry child so that we can move right into spoiling our grand-boys?

Probably.

Been on hold lately?

It's tax time after all….

So, the government says I will be on hold for two hours…. TWO HOURS. Now, I don't get too bummed about being on hold, generally. But two hours, really? Can't they hire somebody to answer their phones? It's a pandemic. Lots of people don't have a job. Lots of people would rather help someone with their taxes than sit at home and collect SERB and watch re-runs of T.V. shows. Now, they may rather stay at home and play with their devices, but I don't know about that because I don't have a device. Honestly, I've given up on the latest technology. I didn't buy an 8 track and I didn't buy a beta video system. I think I did the right thing and did not waste my money on those devices and I'm holding out – I won't buy the latest cell phone. My flip phone that I have for emergencies is just fine.

ANYWAY. I'm twenty minutes into the call and I've figured out how to turn the volume down on my land line phone. I can hear the music and the periodic announcements in the background. So far, the classical music with full orchestra is OK. Not my favourite, but OK. I've been on hold before and suffered through some pretty bad music.

Music that is so bad means the "hold" company can't afford anything better. They buy bad music and just repeat it over and over.

I think that Canadian "hold" companies should have to buy Canadian content. They should have to buy different genres as well. Start with the classical music. Have we ever had a classical composer here in Canada? Good, we'll skip classical then, twenty-five minutes into my two-hour call and I'd had enough with the classical. So, we should start with Indigenous music. I love Native North American music. Some good throat singing would be great. Then throw in a Canadian Country tune. Canadian Rock, Canadian folk songs, Canadian Maritime Music. Oh, and I love that West Coast gum boot dancing music with the sound of the gum boots in the background! Ukulele music (I know it's not originally from Canada, but I actually play the ukulele...), Oh and hip hop if you think it necessary – it's only seniors that have time for being on hold and they may not like the latest in that genre – the latest commercials seem to need that music. That could be enough for Seniors. TWO HOURS of hip hop may not go over well on the hold call... EH?! But maybe that's the secret intention, tick off as many people as you can and you can cut down on the hold people so that the

Government of Canada doesn't have to hire anyone. GOT IT.

Wait, oh no, my phone is beeping. If it dies, I have to start again...

Part two....

So, the reason I was calling the government was to change my dad's address for tax purposes. That was why I phoned. I tried on line, but there were passcodes I didn't have. I was on hold for THREE HOURS and was told that I couldn't change his address. When I explained that Dad was 92 and could NOT be on hold for three hours and was too deaf to even understand the process, the girl went to find out more info. She said I could print the form on turbo tax and send it in. Turbo tax said I could NOT print it and send it in. So, the girl went to find that out (didn't I already tell her that?) and then the call was dropped!

That's my fun for today - if you had more fun than I did, please let me know!

Susan Carter

Sixty-five

Today I turned sixty-five. I thought it would be a good idea to warn all those well wishers on Face book, so I posted my new photo and the information that this Ground Hog wouldn't be looking for her shadow, but would be worrying about her new Senior Status.

I started the day happy that I didn't get a sub job – it's hard to explain how old you are if you are teaching little kids. Then my own personal Curmudgeon came to ask if I wanted to go out for lunch or supper. The information he regaled me with was that we were supposed to get a flash flood later and it would be a good idea to go out for lunch so that we could avoid the flash flood thing and also, we could avoid the drive after dark. OK, lunch it was. We went to our new Thai place that's all of a sudden getting popular. We got a space to eat, but we didn't arrive in time to get chairs, just stools. So, there was no time for appetizers or dessert because the Little Man's back started to heave when we finished the main course. I decided to not get my favourite meal today, I may be 65, but I do love an adventure. I ordered something that came with a strange tasting seaweed-like green food. This green food was very hard to bite, and – very hard to swallow. The meal otherwise tasted good. I was full, but I asked for my favourite ginger tea to go, but they can't do that tea in a to-go cup, only in a pot. OK... Bummer.

We came home to hear the four-year-old twins sing happy birthday on the message machine. I saved that of course, because I can re-play and get tearful at another time. But not today, I was getting heart burn and I needed a nap.

Sixty-five isn't bad, I'm doing everything I have always done – and in between naps I believe it too!

At my age it's prune juice

Shoes Suck

Or: Questions

Grey leather they were
Perfect fit
Perfect look
With three small black patent circl-y insets
Perfect price – three dollars
Brand new
Perfect heel
Did I mention Perfect fit?
My dream shoes from the Army and Navy
Regina, Saskatchewan

1973
Was the last time
Everything came together
In my shoe universe

Now I dread shoe shopping
Heels too high
No room for toes, and

My heel slipping out of
A too wide back

Size 8 too small, size
9 too big
I fantasize that
If there was a size 8 ½
It would lovingly surround my orthopedic
Lifts and make these
99 dollar fake leather
With the sauna-like lining
Ugly
Clunky
Shoes
Actually fit

Did Cinderella have
Foot problems?
Is that why no one else could
Cram those glass slippers on?
Should I have cut 2 toes off in 1973
In order to wear fashionable shoes?
Can you find Prince Charming
Barefoot?
And if you did find him
Would he have been funny?

Susan Carter

Climate Concerns

I've had many questions over the years about helping our planet, but no one in the media or politics deals with the small picture, instead they worry about global everything. I worry about global everything, but I realize there are some things I can do on my own. I would really like to have a T.V. or radio show with helpful suggestions, so at least I can feel like I'm doing something, even though most of the things I am working on and will continue to work on seem small.... If I knew how to do a podcast, perhaps that would be the thing, I do know how to type so here are the questions I would ask my imaginary podcast guests...

- Letter writing seems like a good idea – even though this does waste paper will the corporation I write recycle after they reject my idea?
- Not buying non-recyclable anything is a good idea; are the grocery stores on board?
- Who makes the decisions to bleach diapers, toilet paper, feminine hygiene products, and elderly diapers?

- Where can we get solar products for our house and, if we do get solar, what happens – do we fill batteries, or can we hook up to our grid?
- What government is working on solar, helping out the "poor" people to install? If I ever find a person willing to do this, I will vote for them.
- What modes of heating our homes is the most efficient and beneficial to the planet?
- Why does every public building air condition their buildings to the point where I never wear summer clothing because I would freeze? I get a little warm running from my air-conditioned car to the public building, but that's minor, I drive around until I waste enough gas to get close to said building...
- Who do I write to find out where our recyclables are going? Are they innovating new ways of disposing of it? Are "they" shipping to another country to ruin their environment? That was a good one – pretend to be concerned about our environment to ruin some other country's environment.
- Do LED lights actually run longer? I've been disappointed in the ones I buy.
- Will flushable cat litter clog up the waste water system?
- How come Tim Horton's coffee tastes better out of that non-recyclable cup than if I brew it at home?

Help me out here... do some small things with me... or get me an interview on a major network... I'm too old to start podcasting.

Poem for the Environment

Save the planet by not going outside

Watch wildlife documentaries on TV

What, is it discovery?

You'll never trample anything that's endangered

If you stay inside,

You won't be bitten by... well anything!

You can use your time inside to recycle

Those boxes Amazon sent you

Sorry I wrote this out, I'll recycle the paper...

Promise

After driving across Canada to retire....

July 2009

Week 1

Well, here we are, I can't believe we made it. Minor fighting along the way, nothing serious, just a few disputes about road signs. I must say, I was right most of the time. If you have the job of navigator, you also have the job of pointing out to all who will listen that the driver.... well, didn't listen!

We were happy that the weather was rainy and cloudy the whole way; it was easier driving, no cooked bodies stuck to the windows of the van.

Wow, it is so quiet here in rural Nova Scotia! I heard a noise tonight, just realizing that it was a moth beating himself up to visit me. Then I look up again and there's a cat wondering - still up after curfew.... It also seems very dark on our street – after the excitement of

99th Avenue and Dairy Queen in Fort Saskatchewan, Alberta.... I never thought to mention it before, but Alan's snoring keeps me sane...

We actually arrived July 7th later in the day. We were thrilled with the garage (not done, but thrilled so far); BUT not so thrilled with the state of the house. I had been happily looking forward to all the cupboards we have in the kitchen... I wasn't happy vacuuming and scrubbing them all out! Also chucking out the CRAP left behind – it was like playing a game show, what's behind door number 2 ---------- EEEW!!!

So, it took 3 days to clean the cupboards in the kitchen. Alan couldn't put anything away until ALL the doors had been open and the contents chemically eviscerated. As it is, he is not happy because the door of the stove wasn't on the first 3 day "to do" list. But he bravely soldiered on and the cupboards are just about complete. Soon I'll start washing the ceiling. Spaghetti sauce; I think...

We've been shopping for tons of stuff too.

July 8th the movers arrived first thing. At noon the bedroom and dining room furniture arrive and then at 3 the mattress and box springs were here. Clockwork organization due to Alan, but what a lot of piles! Thursday the washer, dryer, freezer and telephone guys arrive. I just imagine our money evaporating every time there's a delivery!

I discovered a great way to make friends. Buy someone a coffee in the line at Tim Horton's and it gets everyone in the line talking – so buying friends is now an option. We could put a sign in the window as well.... Wanted, friends, no qualifications necessary! This would replace a security system sticker.

Today we took a break and went shopping! Tomorrow we're going to Halifax; you guessed it, to go shopping!

I went to the Baptist Church up the street today. I needed a rest from all that shopping. No Choir. Just kids on guitars – that seems to be a trend in the Pentecostal type churches. I saw it happening in the Free Methodist Church as well. So, I crossed this church off my list. But I sat and wrote quite a few jokes during the time spent there! To be honest, I didn't like the vibe in that church. I figured out at the end that as a single woman I was a threat! Ha, I certainly don't need to start messing with anyone's husband, it keeps me busy messing with mine!

Shopping alert - We keep running around buying stuff. The American Express is Maxed out and every day the list of things we need to buy gets longer. I don't need anything for the sniper tower - I brought it all! Unfortunately, we keep finding sales and decide we can't do without the whatever.

Last night we went to introduce ourselves to the neighbours. We found out that the sniper tower caused quite a bit of speculation before we came! The second home we visited earned us a glass of wine with the intro... so success for that endeavour. We also found out that the couple previously in the house went through quite the divorce... ahh, that explains a lot!

Week 2

Has been an extension of week 1. I'm still not finished cleaning the kitchen cupboards, but plan to.... We've argued our way to a few purchases, but some arguments are still on going. We now have a bet on how big a particular rug is that we liked. Alan has won some rounds; he has conceded on some as well. We agree that we are spending money like mad. Tonight, we pooled our cash and went out to a Strawberry social that was put on by the Kentville Kinettes. We knew that the price was $9 each so we were fine. Our money has been frozen in my new bank account until the first cheque clears and we didn't have debit set up in the account we have had for five years. So, we were literally broke; although I kept some money for the collection plate at church tomorrow. I'll try the United Church; no choir at the Baptist last week, so I'm moving on.

Last week I applied for a job! The fabric store that I'd discovered on previous trips was looking for part time people. I'll probably hear one way or another the first of the week. This would be a great place to work at while I make curtains for the house!!!

Week 3

I was reading my first two attempts at a weekly diary of the summer for everyone. Fighting and money are a recurring theme – sorry! I'll do better, the fighting is pretty much over because the money is gone!

Yes, Hurricane Bill wasn't much for us here. We are 10 minutes from the Bay of Fundy, but the storm hit the South Shore (where Peggy's cove is) and carried on up to Cape Breton and Newfoundland. The good news is that lots of people called from "out west" to check up on us. The Sniper tower was just completed 3 days ago, it would have been not so funny if the storm had taken it away! (Tower room is 15 x 14 feet with a huge bathroom – I love it)

I talked to a teacher still in the salt mine today and she said that the kids go back to school on August 31 – I vaguely recall all those staff meetings. It's our 35th anniversary; wow the first time in all those years I won't be at school. I plan on going to Tim Horton's and handing out Tim Cards to anyone in line with me – I'd give special ones to teachers, but I won't be up that early....

We are going to Maine on the "Cat" (super fast ferry) for a couple of nights September 2 for an anniversary celebration. AND we've booked a trip to Cuba in December.

Alan and I have had to learn how to recycle. There are two different blue bag options – I haven't figured those out yet. Compost and cardboard are separate. The cardboard has to be cut into same size pieces and tied. You get to have one actual garbage bag... if for some reason you need a second one, all that garbage has to go into a clear bag for inspection. Mind you after recycling everything, there isn't a whole lot of garbage. Each household is limited to a certain number of bags as well. Pick up is every two weeks. The neighbors are very helpful with tips and hints about garbage! The movie theatres and Tim Horton's recycle bins as well. I realize that the Tim Horton cups become garbage because of the plastic coating, so it may just be a Tim Horton ploy...

I got the job at the Fabric store. I made a 50-cent mistake with change the first day – luckily not 50 dollars. I'm working 3 short shifts a week there. I'm on the sub list and I've just started making contacts for comedy.

Alan's back is getting better. He's not talking of golfing yet, but he did take out all the golf equipment and found the missing fridge magnets and the small Inukshuk that was a parting gift from the Alberta Teachers Association. Alan had me convinced that the movers had lost these two items – he had gone through EVERYTHING. The large Inukshuk from my school arrived safely because it rode in the car with us and is in the living room – so I can look at it everyday. Inukshuk was a theme of my retirement. Perhaps my co-workers thought I needed landmarks in my retirement. They do commemorate my time as a classroom teacher.

* *We affectionately called the room on top of the garage the Sniper Tower. I loved that room because it had all my "stuff" in it and I had a great view of the Annapolis Valley. It was called the Sniper Tower because it was up high and we lived close to the base in Greenwood, Nova Scotia. One of the wits I worked with came up with the name Sniper Tower and it stuck. Another parting gift I received was a very large water gun that was on prominent display in the Tower.*

** *We were happy to have gone on that Cat trip because the Cat was retired soon after. We never went to Cuba, I broke my knee-cap. Another story somewhere....*

Susan Carter

Friendships are Amazing

I've been thinking of my friend Barb lately. It's funny how random people from your past, just, well take over a part of your brain. It's like trailers taking over the parking lot at Walmart... only less gas fumes in the air.

When I met Barb, I was teaching. This was my first job teaching. I taught Kindergarten through Grade Eight music. The teaching was four days of the week. I spent the other three days plus evenings learning the songs I needed to teach plus learn Ukulele ("Oh yes, I can teach Ukulele" became a bitter mantra that year). I squeaked out Hot Cross Buns on my recorder with the kids. I don't remember any other songs, just Hot Cross Buns, perhaps we didn't progress very fast on that instrument... it could be I didn't have time to learn more. I got pneumonia in January.

Music teachers, I've since learned, get pneumonia... a lot. My theory is that opening your mouth and throat all day is just a drive through for the pneumonia bugs.

My husband was working at a bank that was a twenty-minute commute from our home in Blenheim, Ontario. I stayed home to fight the bugs. I had a doctor appointment the day I met Barb. Another friend who was going to take me to the doctor phoned to tell me her car wouldn't start that morning. I didn't know what to do until I remembered Barb's house next door always had a plethora of cars parked out front. I knocked on the door and asked Barb if she would mind taking me to the Doctor's. She looked at me for a frosty minute (remember I was outside asking this question) and she said wait. I did and she handed me the keys to one of the Cadillac's. I gratefully took the keys. Barb was dressed in an old sweatshirt with a stain on the front. I thought I had interrupted her meal and caught her in her old clothes... but I had no problem taking the car!

I got over the month-long bout with pneumonia, but I didn't get over the instant friendship that grew from our first meeting. Barb and I often got together for coffee. The four day a week job changed to a one day a week job the next year, so I had lots of time for coffee. Remember, I'd learned the songs the year before. We watched a favourite game show while we had coffee and chatted about lots of things. Barb was the same age as my mom and full of wisdom. She had six children. The four boys were in my age range. The two girls were younger. Barb told me that she'd planned the girls!

Now I'm about the age of Barb when I met her. As I look down at my sweatshirt and see the stain there on my old clothes, I realize that we still have lots in common!

A mother's concern

in the Handbook for Hijackers...

- Make sure to have enough fuel on board the jet you pick to make it to wherever you want to go
- Don't let wires stick out of your backpack/sneakers
- Have your phone pre-dialed so you don't waste time dialing the wrong number to detonate the bomb; did you remember to have me pay your bill?
- Wear a disguise when detonating your bomb – there are cameras everywhere!
- Clean underwear – this is a stressful job
- Did you eat a good breakfast? Plane food isn't good for your allergies. When you get caught that jail food can't be good for you either
- Call me, but NOT while you're working. After you are finished your job, you can call, I've got a list of lawyers.
- I love you... most of the time.

Three ways to Fill time while retired

Or living through a
Pandemic as a senior

#1 Make up stuff to do

I'm so restless when I'm not working, and so guilt laden when I am working. I never get anything done either way. Funny isn't it. We drive ourselves to do so many things and get nothing done. I've decided that instead of making a list for "today", I'm making a list for the next two days. That's retirement for you. When I was working, I used to make a list called "Monday", then cross off Monday and put Tuesday. By Wednesday I'd lost the damn thing. How humiliating to have to ask your husband where your list is – of course he knows where it is. And of course, nothing is crossed off of it, even if the pen is found with it. Then I make a new, neater list with the mechanical pencil, I just can't write with other pencils, and then

I find out that the eraser is a bust on that particular mechanical pencil, so I have to either find a better mechanical pencil, or a white eraser. I've purchased many white erasers only to lose them before I make a mistake. (This just shows how quickly I lose erasers because the mistakes just keep coming!) It took me years to understand what was meant by the writing on my Grandparents' pencils. They had owned a furniture store and gave away promo pencils! On the pencil it said, "You never make a mistake shopping at Robinson's Furniture store. That's why we left the rubber off this pencil." Rubber? I don't get it. There are so many hidden meanings in that message. The first one you need to know is that they were VERY religious.... And that kind of rubber just wasn't part of the message they were trying to send.

#2 Watching T.V.

Now, we could be playing video games, but that particular waste of time wasn't ingrained when we were young. T.V. was! We had a black and white delivered when I was old enough to remember in the late 50's. It was before I went to school. It was a BIG deal to get a T.V. We moved to rural Saskatchewan when I was a delinquent in grade 1... We got one station. CBC. If you didn't want to watch the show, you went to find something else to do. Now I sit in my comfortable chair that allows my legs to elevate and try to find something to watch on the many channels our package gave us. I end up taping true crime stories. I've watched so many that I realize if someone committed a great crime (something that can be really sensationalized) then every true crime show will do their version of it with some other spin. I just delete the show if I instantly know "who done it". I often know the story by a character's face – if I stay awake that long!

#3 Going for appointments

This is not as much fun as it used to be – in the good old days you went to the doctors' offices and just sat there with all the other sick people sneezing on you. You got to read those out-of-date magazines in the waiting room, and heck, you can't even add to your exciting appointment by listening to that one patient calling the doctor a quack. I didn't necessarily disagree.... Now, you just have to stay home and wait for the phone call. What else was I doing, but staying home anyway!

And the Choir Sang on

Tune: and the Band Played On

Tenors and altos, sopranos and bass
And the choir sang on
Sarah would play, no attention we'd pay
But the choir sang on
Our robes are so flappy, we're really not happy
We all look like Michelin men
Each Sunday we're here to awaken your ears
As the choir sings on

Sarah's directions are tricky to follow
But we sing on
"Enunciate, don't breathe mouths open and smile"
But we still sing on
"Sing louder, no softer and hold up your book"
We all are so really confused
Our mouths open wide as we sway side by side
And we still sing on

(Insert Kazoo chorus here)

Susan Carter

The loft is so warm that the women all fan
But we still sing on
We can't fall asleep or we're in trouble deep
So, we still sing on
It's Sarah's birthday so we all want to say
We love and appreciate you
At practice each week on the right notes we squeak
Yes, we still sing on!

Words by Bent/Carter

It was "suggested" to me that I write a song for our favourite choir director's birthday.... Well, it started with a meeting at my house to come up with ideas. The other choir members and I looked at many books and came up with many thoughts; then all of a sudden it was unanimously decided by everyone else that I would write the song AND that it would have a kazoo component...really? Everyone stampeded out the door because it was 8pm and seniors go to bed at 8pm. This initial meeting was in January that year. Sarah's birthday is in May. I had lots of time. One of the anal so called "song writers" kept asking me how the song was going and my standard reply was – lots of time left... I would jot down ideas during choir practice (and of course surreptitiously during church). At the end of April, I went to my friend Erica's with my ideas to start on the song. We had it written in about twenty minutes – plenty of time for a coffee break. I hope you like it.

Aylesford United Church Kazoo Choir:

youtu.be/tUiM4Bli-1I

What do you mean you took my picture?

"Mrs. Carter did you know that you taught me exactly a year ago? It was Yoga class."

Yes, I remember teaching Yoga while subbing at that school a year ago, but I wondered how she knew it was exactly a year ago.

"I took your picture on Instagram."

I didn't know whether to have a hissy fit, explain about privacy, or report her to the office. Instead, I asked to see the picture.

It was nothing that would make a sensation on the internet, so the student and I shared a laugh as I pointed out I was wearing almost the same outfit a year later – everything was the same; except I had gotten a new shirt in the last year...

What a mind-boggling thing all these cameras everywhere are. I have often thought a video camera in my class-room would be a good thing to explain exactly what was said with the right inflections for all to see. MY CAMERA would provide the lead up to the "incident". Principals, Parents and Police could easily see that... well it WAS just a joke!

But I do think that I'm glad I'm not starting as a teacher today. Good luck enforcing those "device" rules.

Grouting the bathroom...

Or: When you're finger nails are worn down, the grouting job is done!

I thought it was a good idea to put tiles around my sink in the new basement bathroom. I tried to decide if the whole wall needed tile or just around the sink. After much thought I decided to do eight tile squares – just enough to surround the sink and go under the towel bar. The tiles would prevent water streaks I thought. I spend a lot of time just thinking, but in my mind, I had a great vision of what I wanted. So...I phoned a handy friend, Jon who said he'd installed tile before. I asked him how he wanted to charge me for the job. The choices I gave him were, one, by the hour, two by the job, and three by the Valley. He looked puzzled by the Valley reference. I explained that a lot of people here in the Annapolis Valley don't specify by the hour or by the job, they just fob you off for insulting them by asking. Then these clever Valley people inform you of a price – sometimes months later. By that time, you (the hirer) have forgotten what the hire-ee told you or didn't tell you and hand over what you think is a price that is rather overinflated. You realize that you didn't ask the right questions months ago and of course have no proof that you have been slightly ripped off. You are never majorly ripped off, only slightly. We take pride in the Valley in our recycling programme, so a paper estimate is never used.

ANYWAY... Jon chose by the hour and "we" started the job. He asked me if I wanted wood trim around the tile since it would end in the middle of the wall. "Oh no," I said. So, a date was set for him to come over and he installed the tile where I wanted it. UNFORTUNATELY, Home Hardware had one bad container of grout. UNFORTUNATELY, we got it. When I came home the day the grout went on my husband told me it looked good. I went to look and was horrified to see six holes surrounding each tile. The tiles I'd chosen to install were what someone called penny tiles. So, small round tiles with holes – a gazillion holes. I called Jon. He came over and took a picture of the tiles with holes. He took the container of bad grout back to Home Hardware and the people working there told him they had never seen that before. Now, I've never found this information comforting. But they did give us a new container of grout. Jon reapplied grout as I watched the technique and didn't charge for it. Thanks Jon. Then I realized I wanted to apply another layer of grout because the sink holes sunk during the second application and number three was needed. This was when I realized that finger nails are very useful if you want the grout to be level and the penny tiles to look like pennies instead of irregular lumps hidden behind too much grout. I took Christmas Break to avoid the rest of the job. Then finally in mid-January I decided to get at it. As I thought through what I would do, I decided I SHOULD have opted for the wood trim. Jon did his best, but the edges looked rough. Plus, the vertical edge hadn't been plumbed and there was a half inch discrepancy between top and bottom. So... here's my seven-day fix. Remember, I'm old and am only capable of doing one job a day. We have to save the body for the next project!

- Wash the wall under the tiles. The three layers of grout had leaked and white- washed the blue wall. I SHOULD have opted for the wood trim. Paint a layer of blue over the white tinted parts of the wall. Wash the brushes.

- I SHOULD have opted for the wood trim. Cut and paint the wood trim I bought at Home Hardware. Paint twice. Wash the brushes.

- Glue the wood to the walls. Plumb to make sure it was straight vertically. I use a spool of thread. It's a great tool. Wait for the glue to dry then stand back and realize the bottom of the horizontal wood is crooked. Wrestle with the wood to make it look straight. I SHOULD have actually used the level I brought into the bathroom with me.

- Grout for the fourth time. Realize that there is too much grout and not enough tile in the half inch discrepancy. At eleven at night, I find the X-acto knife and cut four small circles to put in four new tiles. As I'm gluing them in at midnight, I hope that wood glue will work on tile because Home Hardware isn't picking up my calls anymore... maybe it was the grout rant, or maybe nobody works at Home Hardware at midnight?
- Grout around the four tiles and start picking at the grout with my finger nails to even it up. This works best if it's wet.
- Sand and paint the wood trim – the finger nails worked too well on the trim. Wash the brushes.
- Clean up the bathroom. I SHOULD have opted for the wood trim.
- Take the picture!

Double News

April 18, 2013

Good morning from the Sniper Tower! It's a beautiful day here – finally.

We have mega news! Kristel is pregnant with TWINS! She and I had a long talk about the difficulties of getting pregnant while we were driving to Red Deer in February. We chatted about all the pregnancy trivia I'd learned while teaching Health... During the sad day of Mom's funeral, Kristel received a text from her doctor to let her know she was pregnant. She announced to the family the day after the funeral. As Dad said, "You've made my day".

This week she and Joe went for the first ultra sound and found out about the twin thing. She had told me they weren't going to find out sex, so I had been making both boy and girl-themed receiving blankets and of course I was having a fun time buying quilt supplies. I'd also volunteered to make diapers. Now this week, I've done the math on diapers – I would need to make 240 diapers (5 sizes X 24 X 2 if the internet is to be believed on how many you need) minus the 4 I've made already = 236! After an urgent e mail to Kristel, she said diaper service is the way to go – I get to make diaper covers only! AND I'll wait on the colour choices for quilts!

And as this is a news update letter, we have put our house on the market (who won that bet on how soon we'd be moving again?). There are many reasons. Alan and I have talked about moving to a town up the road for a while. There's absolutely NOTHING to walk to in Aylesford. Alan has shoulder problems and likely won't be able to golf this year, so a move will keep him busy... BUT, if we don't get our price we won't go because we can't afford to go into debt over this and I've put my foot down saying that I can't be counted on for substitute teaching money. I want to phase out of that. Eventually we do want to move to Berwick because there's a library, 3 coffee shops, 2 grocery stores and a quilt guild! It's another 10 minutes away from my fabric store job, but we would be closer to the bus line if we get the place we want.

I will miss my Sniper Tower. I only had one piece of furniture I wanted to buy to complete it, but that's on hold now! I believe in keeping Alan busy – moving definitely keeps him busy. He believes in downsizing me – moving definitely downsizes me!

Babies are due in November, so we'll be in Alberta for a visit at the end of the year regardless of moves.

Boys!

Volunteering
means never having to say you're sorry

Recently I became involved in "A Scrooges Tale" – a play put on by our Church. When the call was put out for actors, I said that I wouldn't act in it because it involved memorization. Silly me I decided to sing in the chorus. This play is a musical and the chorus had to learn and memorize sixty-five pages... oops, bad decision on my part.

I spent hours memorizing the seven songs we have to perform.

I also volunteer to sing in the Church Choir

I DO NOT volunteer to bake. I hate baking, I mess up anything with more than 5 ingredients; and I have never figured out if my oven runs hot or cold. The oven thermometer I purchased probably runs hot or cold too. Duc to my bad attitude baked goods are always scarce at my house.

The women of the church spend hours baking, organizing and gossiping. I'm sure I am the subject of my share of this gossip, but I never hear it because I'm never at the church cooking for the big fund-raising dinners, or the big fund-raising pie-making marathons that occur.... Plus, I'm going deaf and seriously; I never hear... because I can't hear!

So, the other night at one of our many practices for the play (love the play by the way, love the songs too and I'm happy to be there), one of our choir members sneezed at a totally inappropriate moment and caused much inappropriate laughter. We were "chastised" for this... at the time and after the practice was over. The sneezer apologized more than once. She only sneezed... everyone ELSE laughed... And I started thinking. Sneezer, you've faithfully come to every practice, you've learned all the songs, and you still feel you have to apologize?

Something's wrong here. The people who should be apologizing are the ones who live their own life and never give of their time or their wallets... or need I say in these coming to be politically correct times, never apologize for their inappropriate behavior or comments....

In the technical rehearsal I brought in fizzy water. In hind sight I realize that WAS a mistake. When the lights went down, I opened the drink quietly. Unfortunately, the drink had rattled around in my car on the way to practice (I volunteer my gas/car as well) and we ended up with a fizzy fountain. Since we'd been told we couldn't laugh, we killed ourselves silently as I tried to put the lid back on the drink. Due to this mis-hap, I missed the timing for my bell ringing. I was chastised. I explained that I was having technical difficulties.... But I refused to apologize... Volunteering means never having to say you're sorry! This is my new mantra.

*I had such a good time doing this musical. So many great memories. The play was written by our Minister, John Moses.

Susan Carter

Little things that prove you are now a senior...

1. There's something wrong with your toe nail. And so, it begins... Just the big toe nails mind you. While you're sitting on the toilet you notice that there's a white streak running down the side of your left big toe. Whoa – what the heck is that? I didn't know when I first noticed this little annoyance. I don't remember the year I first noticed the anomaly... but I do remember the white streak got wider (about ¼ the width of my toe nail) and longer – it nearly reached the bottom of the nail. Then the other toe nail gets it too. Is this catching, you say? No. Six months ago, I was talking to a foot person. She told me that these white streaks were typically something that happens to basketball players when they stop and start during play and the big toe hits the inside of the shoe repeatedly. So... why do seniors get this same "injury"? Probably because we spend so much time stopping and

starting – trying to remember why we went to the Living Room... The solution she told me was to cut the big toe nails close and make the nail square on the end. Because I know that I met her six months ago and got religious about my big toe nail cutting habits; I know that the vast improvement in toe nails is due to this cure. I have no white on my right toe and the left one has only a third of what it did. So, in three MORE months, I'm hoping to have normal toe nails!

2. I spend every evening tweezing out chin hair – my Great Grandmother gave me whisker burn every time she kissed me – enough said?

3. Your every waking moment is spent avoiding scratching your dry skin. You drink at least a litre of water a day. You ask the pharmacist for their under the counter moisturizer. You peruse the internet looking for cures for itchy skin to mixed reviews. Perhaps you have to up the water intake, try one more internet moisturizer, or wait until spring for a reprieve.

4. You ask the hairdresser what the heck happened to your hair. It feels like straw all of a sudden. What does she mean I have to spend my pension money on conditioner (moisturizer for your hair)

5. What are these brown spots on my hands, and now, face? Liver spots and age spots young people call them. When you reach my age that is an ageist slur! In case YOU haven't looked it up on

Google, here are all the names for brown spots on the skin; freckles, seborrhoeicketatoses, melasma (pigmentary disorder), lentigo, and of course the scary one; lentiginous melanoma. The second one on the list is senile warts! My favourite now! Do you have to be senile? Could you NOT be senile and just call them warts?

6. Did you ever put a band aid on the side of your ear as a young person? No? Me either, but I'm now putting band aids on the side of my ear in a desperate attempt to mute the bright red beacon that my left ear has become. I don't know what I do in my sleep, but I'm thinking I rub my head back and forth on the pillow – it's like grinding teeth. I've put that stuff on my ear that they put on babies' butts to no avail. The only thing that works is wearing a band aid. How low can you go with this? Help me here...

7. Oh yea, then there's the weight gain thing. Loud sigh here.

I've Worn Everything

Tune: I've Been Everywhere

I was walking along thru a noisy crowded shopping mall
Along came some teens – the kind that always know it all
I overheard one say she was sick of all the styles
And someone should make some new stuff –
a change once in a while
There was nothing left to buy. I couldn't hold my tongue at all
I said "Listen kid – you'd wear it if you only had the gall!"

Chorus:
I've worn everything, kid
I've worn everything, kid
Some fit for a king, kid
Some would make you sing, kid
With clothes, I've had my fling, kid
I've worn everything

Long johns, skimpy thongs, granny panties, Spanx
and such

Susan Carter

Garters, girdles, underwear without a crotch
Training bras, pushup bras, nursing bras, Madonna cones
Pasties, falsies, tassels for the no-touch zones
Camisoles, peepholes, undershirts, panty hose
Depends are coming, I'll be gumming, after that – who know?

(Chorus)

I've worn hot pants, sweat pants, gauchos and pedal pushers
Loose pants, tight jeans, some were real bum crushers
Miniskirts, maxi skirts, a-lines and kilts with pleats
Flip flops, high heels, platforms and some with cleats
V-necks, turtle necks, cardigans and Nehru jackets
Evening gowns, markdowns, lots of stuff with darts and plackets

(Chorus)

I've had long hair, straight hair, French braids, really puffy
Beehives, dread locks, pony tails, short and fluffy
Afros, gizmos, finger waves, corkscrew curls
Home perms, frizzy dos, everything was swirls and twirls
Blunt cuts, buzz cuts, even had a Mullet once
Page boy, teased high, corn rows, what a dunce

(Chorus)

I've worn Banlon, nylon, rayon polyester
Woolens, cottons, sneakers that made me blister
Arnell, Fortrell, pastel, and alpaca

Stripes, checks, dots, plaid, some stuff completely wacko
Seer sucker made me pucker, silks and satins, linen too
Fashions through the decades – Ha! If you only knew!

Chorus:
I've worn everything, kid
I've worn everything, kid
Some fit for a king, kid
Some would make you sing, kid
"We know one thing you've never worn..."
Nope; I've worn everything!

Erica wrote this song after I gave her a list of fashions and the tune – some fashions I've actually worn, some I took a pass on...

Take your passion
and put it to better use

It was Christmas and my husband was waiting in line at the Dollar Store. I was dithering looking at more stuff. A lady, my-age, pushed passed me and bulldozed to the head of the line with major purpose. I was laughing to myself about the lack of apology as I aligned myself with the-little-man in line. This lady had rushed to start yelling at the clerk behind the counter - about the price of her shampoo. There were snatches of the conversation that were apparent to everyone as the "my-age lady" raised her voice in indignation about the fact that she was being charged way too much for this shampoo.

My husband and I were gob-smacked by her indignation and her rudeness over the price of the shampoo. My husband was compelled to apologize to the clerk – really, I don't think it was HIS fault. I think it was MY fault for being in the "my age lady's" way!

Really people! During Christmas time we could perhaps use our passion for better things – re-cycling, helping a charitable cause, visiting/phoning a sick friend, or, smiling at sales clerks making minimum wage who are working to feed their family.

Have a great Christmas and a passion filled New Year!

During the pandemic this lady probably learned to drive a truck...

Why is every butt product white?

I found myself staring at the toilet paper mesmerized by the colour (or for people who have studied art, the absence of colour). I started pondering about the colour white. Why is every paper-type product that touches our butt white?

Diapers are white. I understand that when we were using cloth diapers bleach would get the cloth whiter. But why are paper diaper manufacturers still using bleach? Do babies turn up their tiny noses at unbleached fibers? Does the colour white make the odor of baby poop less disgusting to a parent whose natural inclination is to gag?

The next step in our waste of paper (for women) is the "feminine hygiene product". Why are all those Drug Store products white? Is it an affront to our feminine side to see that rust brown smear on unbleached pads? If you use tampons, do you even look at the formerly white product on the way out? The paper cylinder is white as well.

Now that I'm at the age where senior diapers may be a possibility, I realize that these might be white too. I need to start writing to manufacturers to ask if unbleached butt products could be a possibility... time to save the bleach part of the manufacturing process.

We could start a movement (HA HA!) called white butts are disgusting. Now this might not be the right name, I need a name I can shorten so I can tweet about it. If I was just pondering BUTTS ARE DISGUSTING, it could be BAD. Maybe it could be WHITE BAD or BAD WHITE, but that could suggest some sort of skinhead tendency on my part and of course that's not my intention. UNBAD wouldn't work because it would mean unbleached paper products are bad. HMMM I'm thinking on it... Any suggestions?

TWIN STORY:

My grandsons are so funny. Braden called the cat adorable. How adorable is a four-year-old active boy calling something adorable? I think it's pretty adorable!

I thought I'd end on something adorable instead of just leaving you with BAD bathroom humour.

Experience Counts

When I first heard the Beatles' song When I'm 64; I never thought I'd make it to 64... if I thought about it at all. But, now, here we are, my husband Alan and I. The world of regular work is a memory, raising our daughter is long over, she's done a fine job on her own these last years and started her own family. We face the challenge of getting older as best we can – the adventure of complaining to each other and anyone else who will listen!

I heard a discussion on the radio about what we should call people who are my age and older. Baby Boomers seem to care about this detail. I personally don't care what you call me when I'm not within hearing distance. That hearing distance is getting smaller for me, so pretty much you can call me what you want, "wherever" but after a discussion with Alan, we decided that we would be just known as experienced people. We won't share ALL our experiences, but most of us Experienced People do like to share. We like to share especially when our memory is going. Soon we will be repeating the same story over and over. Now in my experience, there's good and bad to this – it's bad when you remember every word to every story your friend is telling you... but its good when you tell a joke to her and she's heard it before –and still laughs. Pick your friends carefully - my best advice for all ages!

Terror at the Bus Depot

August 22, 2007

f I was writing fiction, I would make the bad guy put the "drop" in a garbage can just before the "bum" who picks up cans on a regular basis goes by – he could remove your evidence for you.

I was taking the 1:30 pm bus from Edmonton to Saskatoon. My husband always gets me to my destination early. I wandered into the depot, bought my ticket and wandered off to the A and W for coffee to wait for the bus.

Suddenly all of us hanging about were told to "get out" of the depot and then as we loitered on the sidewalk were told to "get across the street". Luckily no one was hit by a vehicle as we jay walked to our destination. No one said what was going on – another passenger told me a canister had blown up in the washroom. No one besides the "get out" guy talked to any of the passengers that I saw. Luckily my fellow passengers were very calm and none created problems that I saw.

We stood on the edge of the empty lot across from the bus depot that was a receptacle for needles. Bus depots have a tendency to be a meet and greet for the people who owned the needles, I guessed. Some of us found a needle free spot and sat down. One older lady propped herself on a post. She could not bend over to sit, and she REALLY needed a chair.

We were outside for over and hour and a half. No information, no yellow tape, no port-a-potty, no chairs, and no vouchers for a beer at the Pub across the other street! Luckily it was a nice day. I asked the "get out" guy who was hanging out with the other workers that were smoking and eating snacks if this was the anti-terrorism plan. They laughed and joked "pretty much!"

This year, the city of Edmonton reported that they had spent two point two million dollars on a terrorism plan. Unfortunately, the Bus Depot didn't get a photo copy of the plan. Perhaps some of the two point two million could have been spent on a bull horn to order passengers around, pay someone to check on the comfort of the passengers, or provide a couple of folding chairs for said passengers. Money could be spent to arrange with the Pub for shelter, or at least buy a tarp to protect us from the weather.

When I finally got on the bus, the girl selling (she could have given them for our inconvenience) headphones for the movie was surprised to think that I might want a free drink. The really funny part was the movie – Clear and Present Danger!

To end on a positive note; the bus driver that afternoon did apologize to us for the delay.

The Greyhound service from Edmonton to Saskatoon was discontinued October 31, 2018.

Apple Cider Vinegar cures everything...

Right? I'm learning that ACV is curing my minor – well minor to you – complaints.

The first problem it cured was ring worm. Ring worm you might say, what is that? I know, because that's what I said to the Doctor, I'd never encountered it in the prairies where I used to live. It's an itchy patch on your skin. Ring worm is usually roundish in shape. Do not say round worm though, that's a tropical disease that I'm sure I'll never get because the little man has decided that he may never travel again. I found out I had ring worm when I found I was scratching an area of my butt for what seemed like months. Finally I decided to do gymnastics to see, and there was a raised dry area shaped like a "U". Ringworm is cured according to the doctor by some topical drug to be used until it is gone. The packaging said to not use it for more than a month. The doctor said to use it as long as needed. After a very short time

I started to taste the drug! That's when I researched and found many cures – I chose Apple Cider Vinegar because I happened to have it. When I first applied ACV to the area, there was a burning sensation – this must be good I thought. I never did taste the vinegar and after a while the mark and itch went away. If you don't know, ringworm is supposedly caused by farm animals. I never go to farms, but my cat perhaps does...

So, as a result of this research, I liberally apply ACV after a shower to prevent itch and if any part of my body seems to even THINK about repeated itching, I prevent ring worm by drowning the area a couple of times a day.

So... then I started getting heartburn. Perhaps I'm drinking too much coffee, so I research how to cure heartburn... ACV is one of the ways... WOW, I happen to have a BIG jug of it...

As I get new minor problems, I'll start by treating them with ACV – I'll save a lot of research time that way! Mind you, I always seem to smell like a salad....

Singing in the Shower

I glory in the shower of water
So happy knowing that the
Cleansing water
Here at the Public Swimming Pool
Has no consequence....
I don't have to clean anything up

I glory in the song that echoes
Off the tiles that
Someone else cleaned
When....
The song stops more abruptly than that
Annoying short-lived automatic water tap

Because

I don't glory in the
 Screaming Teens
Chasing each other into my solitary space
The boy hastily backs out

Susan Carter

The girl embarrassingly in front hesitates
She says
"How are you Mrs. Carter?"
My answer is the obvious....
"Naked"

This and That...

If you choose to "come back" as a hair – would you choose a head hair or a hair somewhere else, well if you're male, you would want to come back as a pubic hair because that's where all the action is – AND you would have to worry about being on a bald head spot. Just a thought...

Cooking tips for men:

- Pork and beans aren't a side dish every night
- When cooking vegetables on the stove, add water before you put the parsnip in the pot and walk away
- Chicken liver gruel may not catch on everywhere
- Adding food colouring to pierogi dumpling dough may do the trick of differentiating the fillings... but...
- Frozen pizza is NEVER on my diet!
- When you walk out of the house and have forgotten you were broiling cheese on buns... remember vinegar in bowls around the house removes the

smoke smell. Also remember to send money to your local fire department...

Why are older choir members deaf and blind? We are deaf because the modern microphones that NEED to be used in church squeal. We strain to hear the jokes people make during funerals. People tend to swallow the punch line and the choir tries to ask the one member who still has all their faculties what that punch line was. Perhaps we can get sponsored by a hearing aid company. AND we are blind because the flash cameras are worse than the paparazzi during those Christmas concerts. The parents are taking pictures of their kids dressed as shepherds. I'm sure there are some stats on how many "extras" become shepherds at Christmas concerts.

You know you're old... when the hairdresser says – Boy! The back looks good!

I like animals; if they don't like you, they bite your hand, they don't pretend to like you, THEN bite you – those would be the politicians!

What's with the camouflage jackets with bright orange in them? Are we preparing for Nuclear Winter?

My husband is a boy toy – unfortunately he's sitting on the shelf now, collecting dust!

When I retire, I'm going to get a 1-900 number. Then when the kids phone me, they have to pay for every minute they are begging for money.

What do middle aged women and post pubescent boys have in common; well, we all cut our faces shaving, Oh and of course we think we're funny.

Have you bought any of those soybean garments? Yeah, if you get tired of the outfit, you just boil it and serve it for dinner!

Where does your time go? Have you ever sat down and figured out your day? When you were working, eight hours (or more) was spent there. Four hours is spent getting ready for work, for bed, and for supper. Two hours was housework. Some of the day was for you. Then you slept the rest of the day away. Where did the day go? Now that I'm retired, all of my day is for me and I still wonder where did my day go?

Cell phone for drivers – it has the left- and right-hand signals right on the phone!

The other team is from a rougher prison and they play dirty!

The best day with my daughter was when she told me she would rather shop with me than Dad!

So... I think I want to be an actor. I have the perfect part for me – a baby on those polluting plastic and bleached paper diaper commercials. I can handle being held in someone's arms, sleeping, and not learning any lines. I'm also going blind so I can look nearsightedly at the person holding me in their arms. Although doing two things at once – looking nearsightedly at the person and yawning at the same time might take some time and effort in rehearsals. Do you think they'd hire me when I told them I don't approve of polluting plastic and bleached paper diapers? Ethically, this is tough.

Pessaries

This is a cautionary tale told to seniors – kind of like a faery tale to kids…

When my grandma was in her eighties, she had a hysterectomy. The successful operation happened while she was visiting Edmonton where I was living at the time, so I was told what had happened to her. Her uterus had "dropped". I figured out that this meant some of it had come out of her body – I can best describe it as a bubble of skin that comes so close to the opening that you can feel it.

Are you squeamish yet? Are you a young person saying "this is just gross"?

Well, whatever your reaction is so far, hang in there, I'm giving you very valuable information if you are a woman, and even greater information of you aren't a woman, because you need to be sympathetic, or at least pretend to be sympathetic if this happens to a loved one…

So… when I had the bubble of skin happening to me, I knew it wasn't a growth, I knew it probably wasn't cancer, and I knew that an operation was in my future.

Susan Carter

And as I discuss this condition with other women who have the same problem, the funniest comment was allegedly said by a (unsympathetic) doctor... "It's like a dead chicken coming out of your vagina". Nice...

So, I go into see the gynecologist who tells me I have three choices. The first choice is to live with it, the second is to wear a pessary (spell check has not got this word on its vast list) for the rest of my life and the third is to have the operation. I just can't live with a dead chicken, so I say, well if Grandma can do it, I can do it. I opt for the operation...FYI.

A pessary is "an elastic or rigid device that is inserted into the vagina to support the uterus".

I have no excuses for what happened next. I HEARD the nurse tell me that I should have regular bowel movements in the six-week recovery period, I also heard that I couldn't do any physical work – and that was what I passed on to my husband. Perhaps I should have told him about the bowel movement thing too, because he may have told me that my permanent constipation was NOT a normal state to be in... and I SHOULD HAVE been ingesting every product on the market to soften- up all my bowel products!

So... the operation went fine, and I enjoyed not doing any physical labor for six weeks, and I blithely continued my regular constipated bowel movements. After a few weeks the dead chicken makes its appearance again. I ask the doctor if my uterus had grown back (weak attempt at a joke). He told me I'd done too much physical labour – I knew I hadn't. It was much later that I put this story together. After the doctor and I had calmed down, I was told there WAS NO operation available for "Pelvic organ prolapse". So, I now have TWO choices. The first is... doing nothing, and the second is a pessary for the rest of my life.

Have you got the lesson yet? The lesson is... do everything in your power to pass soft stools when you are recovering from a Hysterectomy and, of course, make your spouse do all the physical labour around the house...

AND... for your entertainment I am including a routine on pessaries so you realize that you DO NOT want one....

https://youtu.be/MtTu_dvBQ-g

Note the nice grouting in the background...

Why Grandmas need potty chairs!

S o our darling daughter (aka DD) produced twins three years ago – YEAH! We were thrilled to have boys since we didn't have a son, TWO grandsons sounded like a great idea. We live in Nova Scotia and our daughter and family live in Alberta. Oh well, that's the way of things these days when people need to look after their financial well – being.

So... we saved our money and went to see our boys for their third birthday. I took the gifts, for the birthday and coming Christmas, bought material to make them their Minion costumes while I was staying there... I thought I had it covered. HA, there's always something you forget...

The boys have been potty trained for a while now, kudos to our DD. As a Double Whammy Grammy, I thought how cute to see the boys standing on a custom made box (kudos to their Dad) to pee. The problem (you knew it was coming) was the once a day (or more) when the boys have to sit on the potty. Most of the time

DD was there to lift them onto the potty. BUT... the one time she was out I was the DPL (designated potty lifter). Aaron, of course the one who weighs the most, had to go. I puzzled out the placement of the potty adaptor and lifted him onto it. I was surprised when he started yelling "help Grandma" in record time. I went in to help with the last job the DPL has – bum wiping. OOPS, there was Aaron slowly sinking into the drink. I grabbed him putting him upright and repositioned the potty adaptor. Now, here is where I should have called Grandpa, no, I worried about accidents and permanent bowel problems for our Aaron – I lifted him on AGAIN. I heard and felt a pop and I went down onto my bad knee! Aaron was shocked at Grandma's groans. It was then I called Grandpa.

Since "the Potty incident" I've had two weeks to struggle out of bed and try to walk normally. I've discovered muscle relaxants and had the back X-ray. I've learned things from this trip to see the Grandchildren. I learned why Grandmas buy potty chairs for their Grandchildren, and I also learned that Aaron will probably be a doctor... he asked me every day I remained with him "How is your back Grandma"?

And the one thing I forgot to do? Obvious now, I forgot to up the weight training before I visited my three year olds.

Would I change anything about the visit? No, of course not, I'm the Double Whammy Grammy!

> # I love coffee shops!

I love the local coffee shop. It is such a customer oriented and loving place! You walk in the door and you get the same service every time. If you order a take-out paper cup, you automatically get two cups so you don't burn yourself and sue - even if you said "one cup please". So, you take off the extra cup to half-save the earth and leave it on the counter. The staff member lovingly takes that cup for you and lovingly pops it into the garbage; another service for you!

If you opt for the china mug because you're going to sit in the Shop and visit or meditate for the ½ hour it takes you to down the brew, you again wait for the predictable ritual to begin. The youth behind the counter grabs the mug by the rim on top so that their "essence" is left for you to drink – yum!

I have my own ritual. I politely ask for the youth to please use the handle as a handle, after all, it was f*##* put on the damn cup to be f*##* used. Oh no, sorry, I only do that in my head, I am way too polite to hurt a young person by asking them to do something so radically new and ground breaking as to have to use the handle on a mug. Instead, I politely ask the youth if they would like me to put my fist down their throat. When they predictably say "huh"? I explain sweetly that since they have in "essence" rammed their fist down MY throat, it's only fair that I ram my fist down THEIRS.

While the youth is pondering over my words of wisdom by continuing the pick-up conversation with another youth working in the shop, I slowly and carefully take my medium black coffee by the fresh-out-of-the-dishwasher-no-flu-symptoms-here-on-the-handle to the cleanest table I can see.

There is a lull in the usually long lineup. I see three employees decorating the walls out of cup throwing range. Only a suggestion here, perhaps one of these employees could have cleaned off the tables before the coffee and new latte espresso sugar rings had dried into multi coloured textural art forms. Oh wait, that's probably not in the manual.

I know how difficult it is to earn minimum wage these days, so I help out. I carefully pull out the one serviette I allow my save-the-earth self to use. I gather spit and discretely use the serviette. The serviette quickly sacrifices itself into a mutilated landfill wad as I scrub off the table. I sip my black coffee on the unaffected area of the mug – just above the handle. I am meditating about how much gas I used leaving my home to luxuriate in a coffee out! I love coffee breaks!

Written before "The pandemic"

Susan Carter

Winter Storms... always fun

Our daughter always wants us to visit during Christmas. Storm season always seemed to start Christmas Day in Nova Scotia. I'm too old to be stuck in an airport somewhere. I was stuck in an airport flying standby over the Labour Day Weekend... once – that was enough. "He" had left town - that ended that relationship!

Preparing for the storm, living through the storm, and cleaning up from the storm seemed to take up a lot of time. We always seemed to have the one respite day, but I chose to not go out. Cabin fever sets in and I always regretted that decision. I got tired of the hat, boots, and mitten routine too.

While living in the Annapolis Valley – our ten-year holiday, I was not prepared for the winter - and sometimes summer - wild weather. The staying home in a storm part was easy when I substitute taught, but when I first came, I worked in a retail store. I was surprised when my supervisor seemed disappointed in me when I phoned in to not work on severe storm days. We lived twenty highway minutes away from the store. The buses weren't running and my husband was pooped shoveling. But retail means always being open apparently. This is a strange statement about our mind set. School boards do close schools when the weather is crappy, some parents and most of the non-teaching public look on this askance – another statement about our mind set. My neighbor next door told her son since she couldn't get work as an EA (Educational Assistant) and he had to stay home he would learn to make biscuits. I loved this learning a new skill at home thing – especially since we got hand delivered homemade still warm biscuits during a lull in the storm!

During a storm we watched the news to see how other people are suffering. This is after the prep routine... Fill the bathtub and water bottles (because

Susan Carter

water coming from our well doesn't work without power... right?), locate candles making sure the matches are in the same vicinity and find the batteries for the radio so you can also listen to the suffering. Oh, and the most important thing to do is call the neighbors who have a fireplace to book our room. I always double checked that they have their bathtub full because I know I'll have to use the toilet if we visit. If the power stayed on, we kept count of the numbers of power outages in the province and thanked Heaven that we didn't live in New Brunswick! After the storms we liked to talk to our friends and compete to see who has heard the worst storm story.

So, the one question I have is... why don't the power companies put more lines underground? This global warming thing is creating these bad storms (fake news I know) and I can't count high enough to guess how much money it takes to hire contract workers to get the power grid outages back up. Prevention seems like a plan I could live with because that seems a GOOD reason to put up the price.

So, I have another question... Who is developing a temporary heat contraption to be used to during storms? I think it would be a good idea to have a little stove that you could vent out a window – like those bedroom air conditioners. You could close up a room to play cards and fool around. I'd buy one!

Enjoy your winter southern holiday if you aren't stuck in an airport!

Wishin and Hopin

Tune: Wishin & Hopin

(Best version is by Dusty Springfield of course)

My girlfriend was trying to get dates on e-harmony
I said honey "you've got to listen to me"
Because that's just old technology!

If you're lookin' to find love you can share
All you gotta do is
Phone him and text him and stalk him
To show him that you care

Show up at his house - *just for him*
Set up the shrine - *just for him*
Burn all his hair - *just for him, 'cause*
You won't get him
Thinkin' and a-prayin'
Wishin' and a-hopin'

She tried to friend him on Facebook
And tweet him on twitter
She even tried that 60 second dating thing, - who could

talk to those guys for 60 seconds
You'll just become bitter

There's just one thing we both regret
We might be too old to be on the bachelorette
All you gotta do is
E mail and text him
you know he's got call display; but hey, those restraining
orders aren't worth the paper they're written on
and stalk him
Yeah, just do it and after you do, you will be his
You will be his
After the jail sentence there's still time...
Actually, it's nice here, crafts, people can't get away when
I'm telling my story; and outside, I hate outside....

*Don't overthink this one... but just so you know, the
words in italics are spoken...

#3091034
Letter to the company that sold me the Sewing table

I recently put together the sewing and design table #3091034. It was quite an experience. I thought I'd pass on some suggestions for you to improve the Assembly instructions... BECAUSE most of us putting together #3091034 are women of "a certain age" who have finally saved up enough money for the table but who have non-carpenter husbands who have said "what do you need that for?" ....

TIME

In the instructions it said that it would take 50 minutes to assemble the table. If I was Snow White and had seven ambidextrous grand children helping me, I could have completed the assembly in less than the 50 minutes. As it was, it took me seven times as long – partly due to the fact that with a twice broken kneecap I can't get to ground level. I know how long it took me because I had to take a break every hour to hit the bathroom, take sustenance, or explain to the little man what was taking so long!

PHOTO AND INSTRUCTION MIS-INFORMATION

- in step 1a and 1b the pictures of pieces "J" and "E" show the magnets (#18) being installed, but the photo doesn't tell a person which way to point the magnets. A clear idea of the direction should be shown.
- in step 1c the picture of piece "I" shows the hinges (#6), but again there is no larger, clearer picture of how the hinges should go on. I put them on wrong, then had to re-do them later (I know, this added to my time, but I'm just saying that the 50 minutes doesn't take into account incompetence on the part of the assemble-person).
- in step 6 the whole idea of tilt-insert was a mystery. Again this would have added time to my assembly as I had to figure "tilt-insert" out.
- in step 8 there are 3 English instructions, and 4 French instructions. Luckily, I could figure out the 4th instruction with my Saskatchewan French knowledge from high school.

EQUIPMENT PROBLEMS

- The open end wrench (#21) didn't fit anything – I struggled to get it to help me put on the casters (#9)
- One hinge had the pin fall out of it when I picked it up (#7)
- The hinges that were on K2 did not function well, they seemed to be stuck. Also that one did not fit into the back of the unit. It helped when I took a razor knife and hacked out some of the wood.

Yours truly,

Of course, my dirty mind quite went in the wrong direction with "tilt-insert". I may be a senior, but I'm not dead...

Here is the e-mail reply from the company:

So glad to hear it!

You certainly brought smiles to many faces around here.

Very sorry though for the struggles you went through.

Have a great day!

Retirement means...

Or: What can I do without a deadline...?

I knew that retirement would be a challenge for me. All those summer holidays had proven to be a very hard time. I was a hamster in a wheel trying to settle down and enjoy something, but in my hamster wheel I was not happy unless I was working. One summer I wrote down how much time I spent at school and just ended up depressing myself. Our financial circumstances at the time did not allow for holidays or expensive "toys", perhaps happiness would not have grown out of those toys and holidays, but there was no opportunity to find out....

When we retired in 2009, my husband and I, for various reasons, decided to move to Nova Scotia. I got a part time job at a fabric store and spent most of my earnings on fabric – when no one is in the store you have a lot of time to plan new projects. After five years working at the store, I realized that I would actually save money (how much fabric can you buy at school?) by substitute teaching. Two weeks working 5 shifts at the store equaled 1 day of subbing. I was an art teacher, what did I know about math... although I'm able to fake it when subbing!

I also continued to work as a stand-up comic and got a few jobs back in Alberta speaking at conventions. I was able to stop in Saskatoon to visit my dad and then come to Alberta to visit with our daughter, her husband and our twin grandsons. The small population of Nova Scotia slowed down my progress in stand-up, but I was able to work with local churches and develop four different shows from the work I'd been doing while I'd been teaching.

In 2019, my husband Alan decided that we had to move back to Alberta to be with our family here because of his health. We had had a ten-year holiday in Nova Scotia that somewhat satisfied my thoughts of "travel". When we returned, I decided to continue subbing, do stand-up for seniors and continue to speak at Alberta Teachers' conventions. My husband was busy joining the local Seniors network here in Leduc, he loves to play cards. I was so happy to send him off to afternoon card games (remember, I don't do math well) while I spread myself thin (i.e., keep running in the hamster wheel) subbing, doing stand-up and speaking. I was very happy to work at something. When I have deadlines to meet, I get lots done.

When the pandemic hit, I was out of the sub game because of Alan's health. Stand up gigs were cancelled, although I did one gig at a senior's center. Everyone had lots of distance around them and masks on. What an experience. People don't laugh when they aren't sitting close together.... And I wasn't sure if they were smiling under the mask, remember the audience were seniors and the wrinkles around their eyes didn't give me good feed-back! Everyone assured me they had a good time, although the laughter feed-back was lacking.

So, the hamster wheel was spinning faster and I wasn't sure what to do. I had dragged many projects with me from Nova Scotia. In the ten years of N.S. retirement I'd made a hundred quilts (mostly lap sized for various charities) and the novelty was a bit thin although at the beginning of the pandemic lots of projects were completed... we are living in a condo and getting those projects out the door gives me more storage space.

I'm still happy teaching, and sharing some helpful nuggets I learned while on the job gives me joy. So, I had applied for Teachers' Conventions as usual last spring and I (foolishly) had checked the box to do virtual sessions. I thought when I applied that it probably wouldn't matter and we would be "back to normal" in February, 2021! Perhaps I was just NOT thinking... I was asked to do nine virtual presentations. Three of them were for a new presentation I hadn't even made up yet. Deadline! This deadline spurred me on to sign up for a course that was three months long. The course helped me with my zoom skills, making up the new presentation, and ideas for marketing.

The worst part of that course is that it's over.

So, after a month of depression – not just due to the course being over, but one cyber bully mean-teacher giving feedback anonymously "Does Susan think she's funny?" I've decided that I'm happiest when I'm working. I'm writing this story to meet a deadline for a magazine contest. I am thinking of the mean-teacher's comment when I include this statement...

No, I don't think I'm funny. I think I see the humour in my life and turn it into stories that lots (not YOU mean-teacher) can identify with and share a smile with me. We are all frustrated during this time of the pandemic, but my BEST days are when I can laugh over something.... Oh, my husband is asking me to "come here.... And bring your finger nails..." Yes... another deadline to meet....

Update... I won a mug for this story...

Susan Carter

Eight-year-old humour

We were having a family game night. It was so much fun to play a game with everyone physically there and no distractions. The game consisted of putting a card in a headband on the top of your head. The object of the game was to figure out the picture that was displayed on your headband. When it was Aaron's turn, he first asked us some general questions... when he got to "Am I something to eat?", we all said no. His next question was, "am I celery?" NO – we questioned him why he would ask that, and he said, "Well, I don't eat celery!"

Braden and his dad were playing street hockey. Braden has been practicing for a while now and even though he's only eight, he seems to be getting quite a few shots into the net. Looked good to Grandma and Grandpa.

Dad was trying to visit with us as the shots kept going into the net. Braden finally got disgusted and said, "Dad! You need to watch a You tube video to learn how to be a goalie!"

All the adults in attendance thought that was funny and we shared a loud laugh. Braden was startled from his dreams of Hockey Fame and said, I made adults laugh!"

It's an amazing thing to get a laugh...

Is the camera on?

I have been doing workshops for teachers for a few years now. When the pandemic arrived, I carried on applying for upcoming engagements, blithely ignoring the fact that "going back to the way we were" may not be an option. I didn't think deeply about the box that I checked off that said... will you do this session virtually? Of course, I'll do it virtually. No problem.

Well, I got a total of nine virtual sessions. OK, what should I do? Taking a class seemed like a good idea. I didn't know the questions to ask, but it seemed to be a good idea. I bought lights, a microphone and upgraded my computer. My ironing board was high enough for me to read secret notes, but not high enough to be on camera. I sewed a back-drop curtain and installed a bar to hold it. A cardboard box from Amazon completed my preparation to dim an unwanted ceiling light/spot light. I had all my art teaching sessions on video on my upgraded computer. I knew how to open them to share with the other art teachers.

The Calgary, Alberta Teacher's Convention offered a series of Q and A sessions to help us speakers with our presentations. I didn't know the questions to ask; so, I used my free Zoom account and sucked all my friends into having virtual coffees with me as I learned how to use Zoom with confidence. I took a session with a guru hired by the Alberta Teacher's Association. I didn't know the question to ask. I thought I was ready. I took the expensive class; and again, I didn't know the questions to ask.

The first session was underway. It was on "stage" at breakfast time. When the first pre recorded art teaching session was rolling, I decided to eat my yogurt. No one can see me as I slurp it down while answering questions on chat. Oh, this is going so well. The second art class was also going well; again, at breakfast time. During the first video, this time I decided to turn the page on my chart "power point" paper presentation. This was a noisy endeavour... but hey, no one can see or hear me... right? – oh dear... that was the question I should have asked.

One of the lovely teachers watching this session typed in the chat... "I wonder if Susan knows we can see and hear her? OH NO. What should I do? Make a joke of it of course.

When I got back on camera, I said... And I licked the bowl too!

More This and That

One night as I was coming home from work, I was trying to see through what I thought was a frosted up-front window – as the frost went away due to the defrost marvel of the car we own, I realized that the blob left on the window was left not by damp air, but by a bird. It was hard to drive down the road with this little gift that of course was planted perfectly at eye level. As the marvellous defroster did its job, the bottom outside of the gift was thawing. I tried to keep my eyes on the road, but the outer rim just kept melting. It was held as a perfect moon shape for quite some time before science took over and the perfect moon shape melted. Watching in fascination did take my attention off the road, but the crazy crap shaped pattern on the windshield was quite something. I was smiling the whole trip making up a story for "why the accident happened"!

I am a true environmentalist. As I listened in horror to the story of all the scientists who are overrunning the Arctic to count polar bears and further stressing them out by putting radio transmitters on the poor things; as you know, I realized I was doing my part for the environment by staying home and watching it all on T.V....

Why do I wake up with music in my head? Why do I hear music every time there is no thoughts or activities to keep my head occupied? Is there a stereo Bose speaker system in my head that some elfin lackey is turning on to slowly drive me crazy? I wouldn't mind so much if any of than music was original and I could sell it on the Internet. I wouldn't mind so much if it was a tune I liked. I wouldn't mind so much if it wasn't that Mini Wheat's commercial. Do you suppose that the person that wrote the commercial was plagued by that damn song as well?

Award shows. What are they, but shows that have rich and famous people patting each other on the back in glittering unflattering gowns? Why can't I go to an award show? There could be a category for sitting on the couch watching TV. There could be a category for wasting time. A category for how many romance novels could be read in a week. Or how many months it takes to actually sweep under the bed. Is there one for how many years it's taken to actually succeed on that diet or that exercise programme. Or if you reverse it, the least number of days a person actually stuck to a New Years Eve resolution. I see many more award shows upcoming as I sit in my glittering unflattering nightgown!

It's snowing nice fluffy flakes – postcard crap for the non-concerned, non-driver. I look at the flakes and think about my accident in the ditch during a similar fluffy flake day. No, I don't like postcards with snow. Oh, the horror of remembering that sinking I-can't-believe-this-is happening feeling as I pirouette into the ditch. Luckily it was filled with snow. My husband congratulated me about this accident. Congratulations on missing the mailboxes and the trees. Yes, when I think of this pirouette into the ditch on snow-laden days I also congratulate myself on living.

NINETEEN DOLLARS a day is the amount of money the Canadian Government started giving me when I turned 65. I am so grateful for the opportunity to get this money as well as spend it! I can buy a lot of Chocolate and Coffee for nineteen dollars! I have always had to earn the money I've gotten over the years, so I look at the nineteen dollars as a lottery win – undeserved, but I'm certainly not going to complain about it!

Covid song

Thank you, Buddy Holly!
Tune: You won't matter anymore

You came along Covid, here am I
Well I'm quarantined so I could sit and cry
Well golly gee what have you done to me
Oh well I guess it doesn't matter anymore

Do you remember Covid two years ago
Back when I had my life – at least I think so
Then, oops – a - daisy, Covid you drove me crazy
But I guess it doesn't matter anymore

There's no use in me a cryin'
I sanitize and wear a mask, now I'm sick of tryin
I've thrown away my nights, safe distanced all my
days ...over you

Well, Covid I'll go my way 'cuz I don't like you
I got that vaccine and the booster too
Please no more variants, Covid then we'll be through

Susan Carter

And you won't matter any more... NO
You won't matter anymore!

Here's the original song on YouTube, I recorded it before vaccines were available...

https://youtu.be/xRachvuYWws

I've been isolated too long

I have an aversion to tattoos. When I was young the tattoos that I saw were on former Service guys. They had blue anchors or crosses on their forearms. I just wasn't impressed by these "works of art". I know, very judgemental of me. As I got to university age, I saw the occasional tattoo, nothing too large, but again, nothing that impresses me. These images were mostly on males, but I noticed that a few very tough women were decorated with tattoos. I was very respectful around these women. I remember that once in the shower room at the pool there weren't enough showers available. I had NO objections when the tough tattoo-d lady wanted to use the one shower that was free. NO problem with me!

I worked in a carpet factory to make money for university way back. One of my fellow workers, also named Susan had a tattoo on her arm that read "Susan and Alan" - I was inspired to say that Alan was the name of my boyfriend (at the time) too! She told me her husband wasn't impressed with it because she'd ditched Alan and married some other guy.

I was channel surfing today and watched, gobsmacked two episodes of Tattoo Nightmares. My mind was bent by the thought of putting a tattoo on my body in the first place, let alone have to go through the process AGAIN to cover it up. The second, cover-up-version involved more skin and way more pain.

I wonder if the other Susan would show up on a future show. I hope I'm not still watching when that happens.

I'm still married to Alan, but still don't have the tattoo.

Many talents vs a few

All my life I've been pulled in many directions because I have many and varied interests. I've thought this was very bad – my brain goes skittering here and there and anything I actually do takes longer because I'm off doing something else very quickly! Some of you out there would call me a "flake" and I'd have to agree.

My husband has always been one to be focused. He will undertake a project and mutter that he will be "happy when this is done". Often, he has to make numerous calls to double check that other people have done their part of his project. If my participation is part of his project, I've realized it's easier to just drop everything else and do my part. Arguments just waste time. He worries about things that never cross my mind because I have too many other projects. I've often thought that "I'm finally done" should be written on his tombstone. Some of you out there would call him organized and a wonderful example to all mankind.... And I'd have to agree.

The last hymn I sang at choir was totally messed up partly due to my fading hearing. Thankfully singing isn't everything in my world. If at some time, perhaps the near distant future, choir will be but a memory. I won't go into deep mourning because I will immediately be on to the next project. My broken arm (December 2016) has healed but it prevents me from doing too much roller cutting of fabric. Oh well, I get the old age pension now, so I bought a piece of technology that will cut various shapes for me! When my quilting/sewing activities are over, I'll go on to another hobby.

I love my husband and he has always fulfilled the role of "the other half" and we have done well together. He has always been an avid sports person. He golfed, played pool, played softball and curled. He curled at a competitive level.

At one time he was stranded many miles (sorry kilometers) from home. He made money playing pool so he could buy gas to get home.

Unfortunately, he now has back problems and he has given up all his physical activities. And, the only project he has left is organizing me...

Do you have many interests and talents, or are you very focused on just one "thing"?

I hate being the one "thing"!

Fifteen things you DO NOT want to say at a 100th birthday party

I wrote this for my Aunt Anita's 100th birthday party. She is a sweetie – well, she recognized me when I came in the door, so of course she's a sweetie! All faculties are firing I'm happy to report (hers not necessarily mine!) If you find any of these amusing, feel free to use them at the next 100th you attend!

- **More cake?** After all this could be your last birthday!
- **How about those Blue Jays?** The person might not like the Blue Jays...
- **Tell me about all the changes you've seen in your life.** This could lead to an early nap by both parties...

- **Are you happy that you're 100?** How does anyone answer that? All I can say is that my aunt has always been happy. I won't tell her that she'll be cranky when she's 101!
- **When your knees bend your eyes close!** This is an in joke made up by Anita – my uncle (her husband) would sit down and immediately go to sleep anytime, anywhere.
- **Has it been that long since your Dog died?** This was written by my Dad and I don't know how funny it is...
- **Why CAN'T you get your Driver's Licence back?**
- **How old are your kids?** The kids don't like this one and remember, they paid for this party
- **What do you think about Trump?** Actually, don't ask ANYONE that!
- **Guess who I am?**
- **Are you still drinking that prune juice?**
- **How's the fitness programme going?** She's in better health than you are.
- **What did you have for breakfast?**
- **You're not drooling, are you?**
- **Any regrets?** Yes... I regret that I invited you to my 100th!

Now, the one question you should ask is.... more cake? Because when it comes to 100th birthdays, that's all that matters!

My rider...

I've been working as a speaker and standup comic since 1993. There are many things that I keep thinking I should put into a rider based on actual experiences. Here are my top eleven...

- If I've chosen to donate my time, mileage and expertise at your event; could you please thank me at the end?

- If I've chosen to charge money for my time, mileage and expertise at your event; could you please NOT mention that in your introduction? I know that's a bit of a contradiction, but Oh Well!

- If you've chosen to hire me as a comic, please do not get your "I think I'm so funny when I tell other people's jokes" loud mouth to introduce me. You've hired me to be funny... if you want the loud mouth to perform jokes stolen from the internet, just go to the bar with that person...

- Pay me before I go on stage. I do not want to stand on the edge of the dance floor after the show and wait for the boss with no sense of humour to open her wallet.

- Know someone in the mafia to collect from your agent, you know the one, he collects all the money and is supposed to give you your share of the money after. Better yet, read ALL the fine print in the contract.
- Put the people directly in front of the stage. Do not allow half the auditorium to be between the stage and the audience.
- Provide a microphone in a noisy bar.
- Provide a microphone in a noisy bar (it happened twice).
- If you want feedback about the event... listen to the laughter, not the two people who complained the next day because my bathroom chunk of humour offended them while they were eating!
- When you advertise your gig to hire a comic, don't just write... ten minutes of comedy for a charitable event.... Write everything... you are a big business with lots of money and you have a big bureaucracy that will necessitate four - hour long meetings and I will MC the whole event. This would probably make a difference to how much I charge!
- Make up your mind, do you want cerebral humour? Dirty humour? or Cheap?

GIGS-R-US-SUSAN

Hot Flashes and too much ice cream

I know I'm allergic to milk. I know I'm 54 years old and ought to know better than to over indulge. I KNOW!

Wednesday, we stopped at a roadside stand and bought strawberries. They looked so good. Strawberries just don't sit well without ice cream, right? So, I ignored my inner voice and ate my share of the mostly ice cream with some strawberries. Then I had my writers meeting. I had bullied them into going to the Dairy Queen after the meeting so, again I ignored my inner voice/guts and ordered a medium (inner voice be quiet, that was the medium, HELLO, not the large) I should be good; chocolate sundae.

All was well until bedtime. Then I felt I needed that last ½ chocolate bar in the freezer as well as some cheerios – I have a cholesterol problem, so I ate LOTS of cheerios with milk of course. Then I didn't feel well. My minor milk allergy had changed. I start to sweat. That's normal; my hot flashes are kicking in. I ignore the warmth and shovel in more cheerios. Now I need to go to the bathroom, but this too would be a normal part of my day. As I'm sitting on the throne, the cramps become a third element. Sweating and cramping that are going nowhere lead to light headedness. Brilliant. Maybe I should lay down. I get myself together and go into the dark because my husband is sleeping in the bedroom. I'm rounding the last curve and I think I'll just "fall" onto the bed. I realize that I missed when my hands are numb and I'm wedged into the narrow space between the bed and the deacon's bench. All of a sudden, I'm panting like a dog and rolling with the pain. When my now wide-awake husband peers over the edge of the bed to inquire as to why I'm panting, I have NO idea and can only repeat "I don't know". It was only the next day that I realize my brain had gone to that "special" place… I'd experienced it once before during childbirth.

I do come up with one good idea. "Spray me baby" gets my husband to squirt water on me so I can cool off. Soon I'm retching into the garbage can, thinking how strange the echo is from the inside of a tin garbage can.

I get no sympathy from my 24-year-old daughter. She has heard enough "woof your cookies" stories and is only ½ listening to my sad story. When I get to the spray me baby part, she covers her ears and is saying la-la-la. Her friend is listening to the whole story and while DD is la-la-la-ing suggests that I could be pregnant. Luckily this is the next day and I'm not hurting... I laugh realizing that hot flashes are not part of their world.

Susan Carter

Will you still love me tomorrow?

Tune: Will you still love me tomorrow?

Last month I smashed up our brand-new car
I hadn't backed it up very far
That sign it jumped out of nowhere to hit me
Honey, will you still love me tomorrow?

Should I tell Tim Horton's about it?
Their sign was strong, our bumper wasn't
It was inclement weather; I'm a coward, so I just drove away
Honey, will they still serve us coffee tomorrow?

Do we have money to pay for fixing?
Should I plead insanity on the witness stand?
Should I have hit the sign just a few more hundred times?
Then forever from Tim Horton's be banned?

We paid extra for air conditionin'
We scraped and saved just to put it in

The way the back window is gaping, we have more
than what we paid for
Honey, will you still love me tomorrow?
I love YOU!
Honey will you still love me tomorrow?

*Husband Alan was visiting friends in Ontario. I had
taken our daughter... somewhere she needed to go in a
neighboring town. It was raining very hard. After I picked
up coffee at TH's, I inadvertently started to turn the wrong
way onto a busy street. Realizing my mistake, I backed up
and hit the sign. After seeing the big hole in the back of
the vehicle, I thought about calling Alan and confessing.
I was waffling... I thought maybe I'd call the next day....
But he must have known, he called ME that night. When
he asked how I was doing, I told the story. At the end
of my maybe-not-so-truthful telling of the tale, Alan was
blaming TH's for putting the sign where they did. I sat
down and wrote this song... emailed it to the friends and
had them sing it to him as they drove him to the plane...

Susan Carter

Procrastination

seems to be my mantra

I do a whole lot of thinking but very little doing

What is causing my procrastination (i.e., laziness)? Perhaps it's because I don't have any chores that HAVE to be done each day. I don't clean; we made the decision to hire a very nice lady to do this for us. I don't cook; if I wait long enough, Alan gets hungry and makes something and calls me to eat. I don't have to work because we have enough money from our retirement to pay the necessary bills. I don't look after grandchildren because they are thousands of miles away. I don't look after parents because my dad is very independent and... thousands of miles away. Fear used to get me up and going when I was teaching Junior High – fear of being late, fear of not finishing marks to hand in on time (believe it or not, I was in fear of the secretary more than anyone else on our school staff!) – fear of standing in front of thirty-too-many grade eights with not enough content to use up the forty-minute lesson.

So, I ponder the question of why I have no drive - is that because I didn't have a crappy childhood? I didn't have any particular physical trauma, I was never treated poorly by a spouse, I didn't seem to have been affected by bullying. Perhaps that's because I have a wonderful ability to kick a lot of my worries into the closet I have in my head – it's a very messy closet, but seems to be holding everything because the door seems to shut everything in.

2018 is four days old and I've accomplished pretty much nothing of note. Nothing on any of my lists. I watch too many true-crime shows. I drink too much coffee. I talk too much on the phone. A major snow storm has hit us now. People are calling to see how we are. Maybe that's why we moved to the Maritimes – to get attention from our friends?

Lovely childhoods do not prepare people for our get-ahead-world. After watching all those true crime shows on T.V., I know that lovely childhoods don't make you angry enough to work sixteen-hour days or commit crimes.

Disease of the month club has been formed (by me) to deal with all the minor ailments that have come to my body since retirement. Honestly. I didn't know I had so much wrong with me until I had time to see the doctors and find out! Now it's an ongoing thing. If I had more time, I would have disease of the week, or maybe disease of the day. But I still have to do other things... watch TV, argue with my husband, curse at politicians, and complain about the rising price of everything!

And, why is it doctors know more about your sex life than your husband? Do they have a special class in university that analyzes the need to know about your sex life? Is there some reason they need to know about your sex life; is it the secret to longevity or is it that all doctors don't have time to indulge themselves; they have to hear about you???

I have found out about a new disease this month – Meniere's Disease. Wow, I get very dizzy and nauseous. Sometimes I actually "talk" to the toilet. Sometimes I lay down and stay very, very still. Sometimes this happens for five days in a row. This weird condition strikes at random times. The doctor told me that it had something to do with my inner ear. And, I'm going deaf as well. Now having this weird disease is like being drunk in my younger days, only not as much fun.

After suffering from this disease for a while, I find out there are certain "triggers". One of the triggers is alcohol. I had one drink at Christmas and was in bed for the five days! The other trigger is August in the Maritimes. The hot, humid weather finally wears me down and again, I'm in bed for some time.

It's just a way of life, you are retired and you have time to think (over think?) lots of new symptoms. Do you take the pills or not? Do you go to the doctor over everything? Not seeing a medical quack for a month is OK, you can still be a member.

The rules to my disease of the month are simple. If you go see some kind of health care person (your choice) at least once a month, you are a gold card member. You know you're a senior if you are a member of my disease of the month club!

*After moving "back West", I have not had another Meniers attack. I'm thinking it was the high humidity and *heat that was the worst for me. If I was doing scientific experiments, I would try out experimenting on people who change climates in their old age.*

Mom's Stroke

April 28, 1995

April 28 was my mom and dad's anniversary; Mom woke up to find most of her sight gone – after weeks of tests we found out nothing could be done to restore her sight – she has peripheral vision on her right side, but no vision to her left.

After six months of steroid treatments that weakened Mom and left her very frustrated because she couldn't work as hard as she always did, I knew she was getting better when she told me she really liked having her white cane from CNIB because in the mall people didn't come up on her blind side, great!

And then she said, "Oh by the way, I renewed my driver's license because I just might have to relieve your dad when he's driving us to Phoenix!"

Really Mom?

> # Quit reading your book in that handicapped stall people!

My friend told me that using the term "handicapped" was politically incorrect. So, I tried to figure out a phrase that I could remember and made some sense. Disabled toilets didn't work for me, because if the toilet is disabled it wouldn't flush, right? The same thought process came to mind with handicap toilets. Comfort height toilet seemed good, but hey, what's comfortable to me may not be comfortable to someone else. Restricted mobility stall sounds good, but will I remember that? Probably not. Standing challenged is another possibility that Google provided, but maybe sexist...? Should I just draw in the little wheelchair?

When you read the following original article that I wrote in 2009, forgive my political incorrectness. If

I change the wording, it loses my original passion for the subject.... Here's the original rant...

Ok, ok, I'll probably only be handicapped for a while, but hey, while I am handicapped, I need to vent about the condition. Some people are really nice, they take the time to open the washroom door for you; then, because they are able bodied, they race ahead of you to grab the handicapped stall; does this make sense?

I am amazed that people actually spend time in the handicapped stall in a bathroom to have their bowel movement. Now I'm not talking about us handicapped people, no, I'm talking about able-bodied people taking the stall to flush four times and stink up the place while I'm standing waiting for this one stall in the twenty-stall facility. Never mind that I've nearly lost consciousness crawling down to this last stall (the debate is; should the handicapped stall be at the far end so others are less likely to want to walk that far or should the stall be near the door so you can make it...).

I've found that saying really loudly to the others that come into the washroom, "It's OK you go ahead, I'm waiting for the HANDICAPPED stall," sometimes works. I've waited for ten minutes people! I NEED to use that bar to "get down" – seriously! I REALLY need to go too! I've been using all sorts of public toilets and I tell you, if you are in the handicapped, check the seat, I really think sickos like to mess with our minds by letting the screws go on the seat so that you get caught between the half moon defective seat and the porcelain bowl when it goes sideways. These same sickos know that when you're handicapped you can't jump up very fast. Bruises and infections form before I can manage to get off the toilet!

The other dilemma I've encountered is the little handicapped button that automatically opens doors when there's no one around to push past you to the toilet. Now, you need to use these buttons because I have been caught in a door while I was in the wheelchair (yes, trying to use another toilet). These doors open very s-l-o-w-l-y. Another sicko designed this; perhaps he wants all handicapped people to die in the fire because they will surely be trampled to death by the mob – the ones coming out of the toilet!

*I broke my left kneecap and went through a year of pain before the doctor broke it again (by accident he said)? It finally healed after another year of using the handicapped toilet!

Susan Carter

Questions Seniors should quit asking each other

There are many questions seniors need to quit asking each other. One obvious one is "How are you?" You could get a graphic report on their latest operation, their spouse's operation, or depressing information about a specific body part genetic degeneration. Once people pass that magic age of sixty-five, they feel all filters are off on the state of their health and they refuse to answer "fine".

- What was your graduating mark from High School?
- Who cares? Who can remember?
- What initials are by your name? – DR – MS – MISS – MR – ADHD?

The initials that I should put by my name are B.Ed. I thought that writing bed by my name was a bit suggestive when I was younger. Then when I taught Sex Ed, I found it ironic; but not something to share with students OR their parents. There comes a day when none of our titles are important except Grandma and Grandpa!

This brings up the next question... How are the Grandchildren?

Nobody has time to listen to an hour (plus) dissertation with photos about someone else's grand-kids. The one exception is if you are talking to the other grandparents of your own grandchildren. They have more information because they live closer to the kids than you do.

What do you do?

The answer is "Nothing". Well, that's MY answer. I'm retired. I can sit and do nothing all day – if I want to! Or, again with senior health problems, there's a long-winded answer. You especially don't want to ask a person who is living alone. NO, because they have no one else to talk to; the answer would keep you up WAY past your bedtime! (8pm)

Susan Carter

I am the very model of a Menopausal Woman

Tune: I am the very model of a modern major general

I am the very model of a Menopausal Woman
Sleeping through the night is an option,
but I get some if I can
I've watched my share of house-
wife shows; Dr. Oz I've just had my fill
When company comes and they ring the bell -
stay very very still

My guilt abounds because Mom and Dad
still live back in our home town
I feel so bad; whatever I do it seems
hard not to let them down
I go to visit when I can
at Christmas and Victoria Day
It's not enough I know it
when Mom says...wait for it... "It's OK"

I thought my kid had left the nest
was making money like the rest
As a mother I thought I was done
had the celebration fest
The phone rings in the middle of the night
what a terrible fright
Mom you're the only one who understands me,
I'm moving home...
WHAT NOW?

Work this week has been full of stress,
computer crashed so many times
Deadlines they are coming up,
but read the e mails they're all in rhymes
Computer geek technologist
fixed it snottily with attitude
Then it crashed again!

I'm thinking I was in a very bad space here...

Susan Carter

I just LOVE all your pictures

Over the years as a loyal friend, I have looked at many photo albums of trips and babies. Other people's pictures give me an instant headache. It is not my best personality trait, but I really can't get into your pictures my friend... I try really hard to look engaged. I try really hard to make appropriate noises, like "nice", "wow", and "awe" in the case of babies. My friends never just hand me the photo album and let me look at it myself. Nope, they want to turn the pages themselves, explaining in detail the "what, where, when, who, why, and HOW" of each and every picture. I've taken to stating when I cross the threshold of a friend's house that I'm only in the area for half an hour before I need to get to the hospital. If food is involved, I can stay a little longer...

But times have changed and with new technology all my old fart friends have "devices" and you don't even have to be at their house, just innocently meeting them for coffee and they whip out the cell phone with pictures of their trips and babies. Does Instagram ("sign in to see photos and videos from friends") mean instant headache – it does for me, again I don't care to see any more pictures. "I have to go to the hospital" is starting to wear thin when there's really nothing wrong with me.

I have spent the last few years NOT opening my Facebook notifications. I've just realized (I'm a little slow) that Facebook is just a giant photo album for trips and babies for people my age. The only advantage to Facebook is that if I duck opening posts, no one notices. They may wonder why I don't comment, wish them "Happy Birthday" or "like" a post if they are deep thinkers, but for the most part I've been getting away with it. I haven't posted about being in the hospital. Hopefully my friends on Facebook haven't noticed. Of course, it all makes me slightly guilty for NOT opening Facebook posts, but hey, I can be a curmudgeon on this, right?

I was doing very well with my eye-rolling crappy attitude on this whole live vicariously picture thing until my daughter decided to get pregnant. Of course, my daughter is special – she had twins. I show people my twin grandson's pictures and I know that everyone should be VERY interested in MY twins, just because they are so cute... awe

Five annoying things about getting older
The Disease of the Month Club yearly update

...Queasy alert for sensitive stomachs...

- So here we are at the end of 2018 – lots of health news this year. The most recent annoying problem was/is the **Cold from Hell**. The doctor said he had patients last year who had the sucker for months. And, unfortunately for me he has been proven correct. I'm in the third month of this snotty little annoyance. The fun part is that a gob of snot will sit midway between my mouth and nose. Great! This usually happens at some inconvenient time. Most times are inconvenient I agree. I was doing a comedy show and every time people laughed, I was trying to hork* it up or out. I never seem to have a Kleenex or hankie with me when needed. You'd think that I'd have gotten into the habit by now. I was driving to teach school the other day and instead of singing along to the radio, I was doing my horking. Because I was alone, I was probably a little more forceful and a gob went flying. Geez... I could have caused an accident as I watched the projectile. As I told my little man this story, I could see his displeasure at the potential damage to the car interior. Not to worry – it was just my pants!

- I'm happy to report that the use of a **loofa** has greatly improved winter dry skin itch – you know the one, it's everywhere. I was never a female to buy into a beauty routine I always said that beauty routines were a waste of time; but as I get older, I realize I'm just lazy. The loofa seems to take the dead skin away everywhere. Works well on the bottom of my feet. Luckily, I'm not ticklish.

- I have rediscovered a product called **Nexcare** (skin crack care). I've woken to a bright red ear most mornings. Some people grind their teeth while they are asleep. I, apparently grind my left ear! This product coats the skin and allows it to heal. BUT don't give into the temptation to pick at this dry coat. If you rip it off, the damage is worse. Mind you it is the Christmas season and Santa may need a reindeer replacement any night now. I used to use the product when my fingers cracked in the cold while I lived "Out West". This was what the product was created for

- The little man has had a persistent cough for two or three years now. He finally got in to talk to a very nice respiratory person. She ruled out COPD and emphysema. She thought it could be a form of asthma so she talked to the doctor who prescribed a new drug (The little man already takes many). So, the money was found to purchase said drug. Two days later he was covered with hives and tried to contact the doctor. We couldn't make an appointment for two weeks. The pharmacist said to quit the drug (duh!). Then he went and sat in a clinic for three hours. They told him not to go home because his throat might swell up. BUT they didn't see him any quicker! He was given new drugs to counteract the reaction. Then when the two weeks are up and he can see the doctor, he will get new drugs to pay for. RATS we didn't think to get that **extended warranty** on the drugs so we could get our money back. Oh well there was probably fine print saying no money would be paid out for allergies!
- My eyebrow hairs are starting to do strange things. Perhaps it's a rebellion of sorts. Four hairs have decided to stick straight UP on my forehead. Luckily my hair is the same colour and I can do that **comb over** thing.

May your health issues just be small annoying ones!

*Spell Check thinks hork is not a word. The words that would be a good fit could be "hark" or "honk". If forced to change the word by spell check - I do like "hock" ... Interesting that spell check DOES like the word "geez".

Seniors put together Ikea Furniture

My memories of Ikea begin when my daughter was three. She loved playing in the ball room there. We were a young family (whatever that means, I'm going with it) and I purchased many items to decorate our home with. Unfortunately, we moved a lot and when I asked my husband where my favourite Ikea wardrobe was after one of our moves, he hesitated before he told me that particle board doesn't survive a fall from the back of a moving truck. Sadly, I know that Ikea furniture explodes when it hits the pavement, but it was too late to revive that wardrobe and I had to console myself with the knowledge that any Ikea furniture that needed to be moved in the future would be tied securely at the FRONT of the pickup truck.

I find reading instructions to put together furniture fun and challenging. My husband grumbles that the instructions are stupid and why couldn't we buy furniture that's already put together. Of course, that doesn't fall into line with my family's inherent cheapness gene.

We once had a contest. We had purchased three pieces of furniture. Two of the pieces were complete with drawers and doors. The third one was a basic cube. In order to give my husband a chance, I gave him the cube to put together. After much grumbling about the fact that he had no instructions (he never uses instructions anyway), he lost. He didn't admit he lost, but the now finished (by my hands) cube was there for all to see.

As we've gotten old and don't have children's rooms to furnish, we've gone to Ikea less and less. We retired to Nova Scotia and sadly the province didn't have an Ikea, BUT when they announced a new store in Halifax, I (not my husband) got so excited, I just had to relive my experiences. We went, we saw, we bought, it was great. I'm including a video to show you how the furniture construction actually went.... Ikea construction for seniors as it were... and before you get mad at me, I do know that Ikea is Swedish!

https://youtu.be/iXkHeDqyBFk

Susan Carter

Garbage picking 101
From your neighbor

April 25, 2020

Hey busy caring people at the Hospital!

During this crisis time, I decided to pick up garbage around our "hood" (since our house is next door). After quite a bit of picking, I thought I'd give you a report of what exactly I found on your grounds...

- One rubber glove – are you really so swamped for gloves that you are only allocated one? Let me know, I'll contribute a box of gloves to you.
- One face mask. Hopefully there weren't any germs/viruses on it... but after grabbing it with my dollar store grabber; I realized that it had been in the parking lot for quite a while...
- The cigarette butts numbered in the hundreds. Wow, I realize that smokers don't have time to

look after their garbage because they are going to die before me, but the most shocking pile of butts was under the Doctors' parking area – EEK! This worries me! We have a shortage of doctors, now I'm figuring out why.

- 1 full bottle of beer...! Alcohol definitely goes with the cigarettes....
- Many fast-food wrappers. These fast-food wrappers aren't just from the local MacDonald outlet. It's a sad state when lots of people – visitors, I'm sure, definitely not your staff, don't have time to find the garbage.
- One loonie. I was so relieved to be paid!
- I'm happy to pick garbage during this time for you and give you my report. Take care.

P.S. The next time I picked garbage I found a jackknife AND the other glove!

P.S.S. I've continued to pick garbage around our hospital over the course of the pandemic. I've picked many more gloves and masks of course. The full bottle of vodka was a surprise... why was it full? There was a satisfying thump when that bottle hit the bottom of the garbage can.

I've talked to hospital workers as I've picked and found out that everyone who smokes hangs around where the doctors park. There's a deeper meaning to this trend, I'm sure. I was puzzled when I found a condom. I found a package of marijuana cigarettes – that didn't puzzle me!

Chicken Soup for the soul (it aint!)

This was written pre-pandemic. I got Covid at the two-year mark, but was only sick one day; not to be controversial but I believe in the vaccinations – I lived through Polio and saw that devastation...

I have the flu. Whenever I have a minor illness, my mind turns to major events. World peace, my own mortality and of course who's making the chicken soup. I've been ill before and when I think about mortality, I think of course of my first lessons in Sunday school about Heaven. Heaven seems to be a reward that is meted out to good people of faith. My family all profess to BE good people of faith, and I can't fault them on this presumption. The family believes strongly in Heaven. It is a place they are going to when life here on earth has ceased. This religious relative bunch believes that Heaven is a better place than earth and they all think that funerals are a celebration of arriving in this better place. At each family funeral I think about the place I'd like to be in when I die and I imagine all the happiness to be attained in that place and all the material things I'm lacking and will achieve in this place. Streets of gold, smiling faces and fountains of, well, chicken soup come to mind – remember I'm sick.

But... then I think of the down side of this Heaven. Will never ending happiness not become boring after a while? Will some of the things that make me happy here on earth need to be replaced? Political gaffes, celebrity babies and my husband's jokes will probably be nonexistent. Will I have to be in shape? Will I finally achieve the perfect looking body? Will I no longer be on a diet? Will chocolate become ho-hum? This Heaven thing is fast becoming a nightmare. And... the worst scenario imaginable; my relatives will BE THERE! They don't come to see me now - what makes me think they would pass me on the streets of gold and say "Hi". And more to the point, what would we say to each other after that "Hi"? I don't want to hear about their perfect children anymore. And I certainly don't want to hear them brag about how God said this and God said that – because of course they would have an "in". No, maybe Heaven is not for me.

Perhaps if I turn Catholic, I could make it to Purgatory. Purgatory could be more interesting than Heaven perhaps.

After two days in bed, I've rejected the Heaven hierarchy. I now start thinking of alternate belief systems. Spirituality of some sort outside of Christianity is a possibility. I'm not up on a lot of other religions, but the Circle of Life idea from Walt Disney sounds good. I think to check with my husband, because if you found your soul mate, perhaps we could do this together...

"So", I say to him, "The next time we are reborn, I want you to come back as the woman".

Because he has been well trained and he was doing something else at the time (heating more chicken soup perhaps), his reply was the usual "Yes dear"

But now we have another problem. I've convinced him to come back as the woman for round two, but for the third time, we both will want to be the man. This chicken soup has elevated my thinking – I have now solved all those philosophical questions of same sex marriage...

I've definitely been sick too long.

Open my eyes that I can see
All politicians who lie to me
There they all are on my T.V.
Wait, I can't watch this, I'm going to pee
RIGHT! now they've upped another fee
Put them in jail, throw away the key
I'd say just roast in hell, wouldn't you agree
But that doesn't rhyme

Open my ears that I may hear
All of that crap, but make it clear
I'm slightly deaf please use this ear
I'd hate to have that good stuff (you said) disappear
S-S-S-Silently now, I just wait for news
Really my friend, I love your views
To open my ears
Illumine me
GOSSIP divine!

Open my mouth that I can say
On second thought, maybe I'll keep it shut....

OR, version two

Open my eyes that I can see
Those tiny notes in the hymn-ary
They're getting smaller can't you see?
A magnifying glass could set me free
Open my eyes that I can see
More than the bulletin - I've read it times three
Please keep them open don't let me snore
Am I the only one that finds this a bore?

But don't open my mouth or I will yawn
Plus I have to visit the john
How much longer will it be
I really, really have to pee...

I started writing this song (verse two) for a fellow choir member who was very upset over some gossip going around the church. If you are puzzled over the spelling of Silently, please see the reference to enunciation in And the Choir Sang on somewhere else in this book...

Flying with West Jet

Berwick, N.S.
March 3, 2018
West Jet
Calgary, Alberta

Dear West Jet Person,

Apologies for my "writing paper". I'm writing this on the plane and did not happen to bring my good stationary, so I used your flimsy napkins!

I'm writing to you to express some concerns about the flight I'm on – flight 1689 going from Edmonton to Hamilton. As I boarded, I was given a new seat. I was moved from 23F to 17F. I was told it was a "better seat". At this point in my flight, I fail to see how it could be "better".

My concern is not exactly about me, but about the gentleman sitting next to me. He came in complaining about HIS seat change – he had booked his seat so he could have more room – he said he had a bad back and he was NOT HAPPY! I wasn't too pleased about his complaints either! He also is a large person, and I agree he could have used more room because my seat was partially used by him. Silly me, I should have put that arm rest down!

When it came time to buckle up, he said he couldn't because the seat belt was too small. This concerned me – in case of an accident, I envisioned being totally pinned down. So, I asked the flight attendant if West Jet had seat belt extenders. She said yes. Silly me, I perhaps should have lived with the thoughts of being totally pinned down – he became very scary in his anger to the attendant... she threatened him with removal from the plane. EEK! As I sit here, I am very quiet so not to upset him.

ANYWAY, that's the story, here are some solutions for your consideration...

- When someone has a seat that suits their physical needs, do NOT move them. Perhaps that could be one of your optional tabs (at no cost) when someone books onto a flight
- Of course, I do not know how the gentleman in 17E was treated when he was given a new boarding pass. But I do know the flight attendant who was probably trying to prevent delays DID NOT ask him about his concerns. Sometimes all we need is some TLC when our concerns are voiced. I do know he wasn't tactful, but...)

- Don't tell me it's a "better seat", because today, it WAS NOT!

Hey guys at West Jet, your job can suck somedays, I know, I taught Junior High for twenty-seven years

The problems of my job drove my decision to do stand-up comedy... I would be HAPPY to help flight attendants deal with problem people – your airline is proud of its humorous approach!

I tried to be funny in this letter...

Yours truly,

Ringo's cross Canada's Adventure

I am sharing the news that Alan and I are leaving Nova Scotia today. We spent ten years here - a ten-year holiday. The decision was made April 18th and it's been a whirl wind of activity ever since.

We drove for 9 hours! Ringo's first hour was NOT good - howling and then he barfed up all those treats we gave him to get him to get into the car. The weather was great for driving - overcast and a little rainy. We found a motel with actual beds! Our last night in Nova Scotia was brutal on the couch in the sun room... The house was clean but the amenities were definitely lacking! Ringo isn't happy in the hotel but like in the car he settled down and has a hidey hole under the bed spread - thinks he's invisible. He might go for a walk with us while on the leash after dark... we'll see.

The best part of the day was Ringo howling in harmony when I was singing "Farewell to Nova Scotia" in the car. Tonight, we're practicing Brother

Susan Carter

John as a round - in French of course as we made it to Quebec!

Day 2 of Ringo's across Canada's moving adventure... Today started with all of us having a mega dose of stress. Alan got up at 2ish. He decided that it was a good time to take his spoiled son for a walk. His mistake was getting me up to put the harness on the cat – so of course I did it wrong. Alan and Ringo went out and the evil desk clerk had booked a very large, very loud dog next door to us. After the dog's noisy greeting, the cat escaped the harness and disappeared into a home owner's hedge. I was in the bathroom thinking of catching a few more hours of shut eye when Alan informed me that Ringo was gone! We went out to call and call and call. Finally realizing the cat's knowledge of Frere Jacque would allow him to make a living as an entertainer in Quebec we were reluctantly thinking of going back to the motel. Alan finally got Ringo to show himself, but he was hesitant to come too close and be grabbed. The miracle continued when no cars were going by at that time as I ran to get the treat bag. After shaking the bag Ringo allowed us to pick him up!

We were all up and pumped so we got into the car and drove... leaving the dog barking in our wake. It was raining, foggy, the highway had many con-struction areas AND Ringo, mega pumped, spent time climbing all over us both. The third time he attempted to scale Alan's head as he (Alan not Ringo) was looking for moose, we stopped and poured drugs into him. He slept the rest of the day. We're stopped in Renfrew Ontario in Motel Room number 2. Hopefully our family is still together in the morning....

Day 3 of Ringo's trip... The day was pretty uneventful as compared to Day 1 and 2. During the night he (Ringo not Alan) got restless at his usual 2am time, but Alan and I refused his plea to go outside... we all remembered the LAST time we felt sorry for the cat... so we caught up on sleep after his two hours of complaining and then got a later start on the day. As we were going through the Algonquin Park, Ringo slept and Alan realized he did not have enough gas to make it to Huntsville. Luckily, we did find a gas station in time. We arrived in Huntsville before noon and will be staying with our friends for two nights. Ringo has the whole basement and has decided to camp out under the guest bed.

Are you all betting on when we will lose Ringo? If you are, please let me know which town or province is your bet!

Day 4 Ringo and Alan took a walk in the middle of the night (IN THE HOUSE NOT OUTSIDE). The big adventure was knocking over a plant, luckily a fake one... I enjoyed the night in a different bedroom and didn't get up for the cat, just woke for the rain. We've been so well fed by Donna that we will be rolling out literally tomorrow am. Ken (Donna's husband) spent the day calling his friends who were old friends of Alan's as well. He told them we were now homeless and one quick witted friend told us that his house had burnt down so we couldn't go there! Tonight we took a proof of life photo – unfortunately Ringo couldn't hang on to the newspaper with the important date on it!

Day 5 of Ringo's across Canada Trip. Alan stressed himself out repacking the car at our friends in Huntsville. After lots of cursing, I do think the pile is a little lower so we can see more of the road behind us. If you want to know, we have one large cat cage, one bowl of water, one jug of extra water, one large litter box, one very large jug of extra cat litter, one bowl of food, two tubs of cat kibbles, two treat bags AND many project bags full of wool because we are trying to help Ringo pick a hobby to fill his time as he goes into semi-retirement in Leduc. He will miss his out all night lifestyle. But all of us have to make adjustments in our later years. Ringo is ten years old. Also, we have the harness that doesn't work, a leash and a collar that so far five people have NOT been able to get apart! Love from Wawa Ontario.

Day 6 of Ringo's across most of Canada Trip - We will have missed Newfoundland, PEI and BC – started very well. Ringo saw a Moose, a Fox and his first Robins (coffee shop) since NS! But the day did start with a major thunderstorm in Wawa that continued as off and on precipitation the rest of the way. We've stopped here at Upsula and they had major storms – the Hotelier guy (I'm saying this very tongue in cheek) said his cell phone was "fried by lightning"? The cat has been very mellow – he's been getting his exercise in the middle of the night leaping from one bed to the other with a few cat cry enquiries about going out the door. Pretty much every door he sees he wants to get out of.

Susan Carter

Alan's day on the other hand has not been so mellow. We got a call on our cell phone to tell us that the movers want to move us in a day early – so we had to phone the realtor and arrange that in Leduc... we've used a lot of minutes of the cell phone on this readjustment of Alan's plans - after we got the room from our surly Hotelier. Oh, and the really bad part of the day was when we never did get into Thunder Bay where we THOUGHT we'd stay the night... I've never seen a provincial map balled up in a fury before... AND did I mention we don't have air conditioning in our lovely room here?

Day 7 of our adventure. Ringo not only leaps from bed to bed in the middle of the night, he also sits on the window ledge. Unfortunately, in Upsala there WAS a window, but no ledge. A very loud WHOMP indicated that Ringo realized there was no ledge last night... just a little late. We did not meet the 2 bears that live behind the motel, nor did we see the 12 moose in the neighbourhood on our way out of town. Now we are overnighting in Portage La Prairie just past Winnipeg. We got a discount on the room here because the AC isn't working. But no humidity here means it's a more comfortable night. Also, I enjoyed my first swim in a long time because there's a pool - makes the no AC worthwhile to me!

Day 8 of our adventure. OOPS... we are criminals! I gave Alan my cool pillowcase (that I'd made) in Upsala. He used it to cool his hot head... BUT when he took the case off the pillow - he captured the existing pillowcase as well. I went to use it tonight and found the stolen pillow case. My favourite hotelier had a wanted poster behind his counter of a customer that had taken 4 pillows, OMG – we will have a poster as well!

I think I'll mail it back anonymously. We are in Saskatoon tonight – way ahead of schedule. So, we'll visit my ninety-year-old Dad for a couple of days. Ringo will again get comfy in a room. He has been so good in the car. He DOES get anxious when we are slowing down. He must think that it took a Hell of a long time to get to the Vet. Then he wants out when we stop - he thinks he's finally home. I tell him soon buddy!

Day 9 of Ringo's almost done adventure. We stayed overnight at the Comfort Inn in Saskatoon. We didn't give Ringo his health food calming meds and I did notice a difference – he seemed very nervous and did throw up in the middle of the night. He was cool all day because he stayed in the Inn. I left to see Dad all day – had coffee after church, watched the Blue Jays (they lost) and then played at the Ukulele Jam – good thing we have two ukes in the car. Ringo didn't want to show off so he declined the chance to play with the group. Actually, he's been off his singing since the "Brother John" thing in Quebec. Alan and Ringo bonded for most of the day, but Alan escaped the room and went and bought a new bed! You just leave him alone for a short time and boom, there goes more money!

Day 10 is the end of the adventure. We left the hotel after breakfast and drove to Leduc. The formerly empty sloughs are full of water and the prairies are lush – compared to some of my years here. All three of us have been catching up on our sleep since we got to our daughter Kristel's. The six-year-old twin grandsons have been very good with the cat they call him "adorable". Marko (the resident cat) has not been so welcoming. There have been a couple of hissing sessions. Ringo doesn't realize HE is the guest. Day 11 was spent trying to register the car and get the mail. I have a whole new comedy act about how you can't get your mailbox key without proof of residence – a piece of mail would do – OH that's in the mail box!

Thank you so much for keeping up with our adventures. If you would like our address and phone number, please e mail me and I will let you know. Sometime next week will probably be when we get a phone number... well as long as we have proof of residence I suppose!

This was written as Facebook posts while we drove from Nova Scotia to Alberta. The cat has travelled more in Canada than a lot of other Canadians!

Susan Carter

Putting Ikea furniture together shows where your marriage is at...

Or... Rules to prevent the divorce

So, I just put together a large, three-door wardrobe, and my marriage didn't have any meltdowns! Wow, things have changed in that department. It's taken years to understand the little man and adapt my snarky behavior to jell our two "unique styles" together to get the right fit (as it were...)!

Do you believe this so far??? If you don't, read on, I'll explain everything in the rules....

Prepare the little man weeks in advance about your desire to purchase your Ikea wardrobe. My guy doesn't instantly agree to my great ideas, so this is a great rule for our whole marriage actually. IF he is well prepared, he doesn't object to putting back seats down in the car and wriggling the three huge boxes between our front seats to get the item home. Just to explain... Preparation means dropping subtle comments about what kind of furniture is needed and where. Expensive versions of the same furniture could be mentioned in the preamble. Expensive hardwood alternatives should be taken into serious consideration while you are in your prep stage. And of course, at the end of the prep period, you should mention that since you are now a senior making over $19.00 a day in Old Age Pension money, you will graciously take the money for the furniture out of YOUR account. Since he didn't see the Ikea part coming at the beginning of the prep period, the price point will tip him over to the sweet spot where he will think it was his idea to go shopping at Ikea himself!

Assure your spouse that you will be putting the whole wardrobe together yourself, but if he has time maybe he could help you put the wardrobe upright. This suggestion can be dropped on the drive home – making sure the little man can hear you on the other side of the Ikea boxes.

Listen to his diatribe on how you should be putting your furniture together. Keep your lips together through this speech (unfortunately it will last the whole drive home   our trip was an hour). Keep a pleasant look on your face and nod your head occasionally – he doesn't need encouragement, just let it peter out. No sense upsetting him now the big hurdle is behind you and you need help getting said three boxes down the stairs.

You don't have to actually DO what he says. Remember all the other times you verbally sparred over the construction portion in the past and how that ended in a Swedish stand-off for many days. His two Canadian cents are worth nothing – he's not an engineer and it took him all day to put that cube together the time you had the great Ikea Race. Remember that you put two pieces of furniture together (with doors and drawers) while he struggled with his cube. Now in his defence, he didn't have any instructions... because he thought they were "stupid" and he threw them out. Today I would not permit him to throw instructions out; they would go in the re-cycle box so I could consult them later.

Once the boxes are in the room the furniture will reside in, remind him that he has missed his cross-word puzzle time and he should get that done as you start constructing.

Now this is the MOST important part to constructing Ikea furniture, do not allow your spouse anywhere near you while you work. YOU are trying to concentrate on your picture instructions and he is telling you how to do it. You will have to break this rule however when you need him to help you get the piece upright or flipped to put the back on. Only allow him to help you when you know exactly what the job is. DO NOT show him the pictures; he again will repeat that the instructions are "stupid". The right thing to do is give him an overview of what you want done, then break it down to simple steps. He will try to give you better ideas, let those ideas float over your head, I listened to one thing he said (I know, I broke my own rule) and I'm still shaking my head over the chip mark I created inside my otherwise perfect wardrobe.

https://youtu.be/SJzH_1zaTv8

Remember that you want the white portion of the back facing inward so that when you open your doors you see white NOT chipboard brown.

Put the furniture together in the room it is intended for. Moving Ikea furniture is a mistake – especially when it falls off the moving truck – it EXPLODES remember? So, sell the furniture with the house. This is a perfect move because if you didn't follow rules one through six, you have the opportunity to try to put NEW furniture together in your new abode. Remember marriage is a long haul not a short trip. AND you get that old age pension for life!

Have plenty of snacks with you. You do not want to get snacks and risk running into the little man while you are working out an Ikea problem – he might come up with a solution that sounds good... BUT... will cause a chip (see number 5).

Don't let anyone know your wardrobe is done until you have it FULL of your stuff and you've made the video! AND of course, covered up the chip.

I love Ikea furniture.

https://youtu.be/a_6iO3RbfZQ

OOPS... after I finished, I found out the leftover hardware belonged on the top. So, I got a ladder and put the screws in myself – never show weakness...

Vaccinations

So, the kids are getting their Covid shots. I understand there's a lot of crying and screaming as part of this process... I sympathise, after being the victim of many shots (and I don't mean alcoholic), I just believe that kids are just not being treated in the right way.

I wasn't yet six and I went with my dad to the Pubic Health Department in Weyburn, Saskatchewan. Dad was training to be a Public Health Inspector, so I thought I was going to go-to-work with him. I was happy to socialize with the Public Health Nurses. One of them asked me if I wanted a bunny or a giraffe on my arm. After deep five-year-old thought, I decided on the bunny option. She painted a bunny on my arm with iodine. Cool. My very own bunny. She asked if I would like to feed the bunny. I didn't need to think very deeply this time; I agreed that the bunny should be fed...

Do you know where this story is going? Dad said that the look on my face was something to behold as my bunny was fed.

I refused to wash my arm for a long time...

Boil Watch
Or... Miscommunication
(Gross alert for the squeamish...)

It was a Thursday when I discovered a huge zit under my arm. Wow! Impressive! After careful examination, I decided it looked like it could possibly be ready to explode, but Thursday wasn't the day. Friday wasn't good either. By Saturday, I was starting to think that this was a VERY unusual zit. It was getting bigger, and so was my concern.

Now you have to understand that my husband and I took the usual marriage vows about sickness and health. Little did I know that the sickness and health thing was THE most important vow that we took. I just was too young and just did not understand. HE apparently chose sickness and I got the health. Even that childbirth thing was easy for me – but hey, don't spread THAT fact around! On Saturday, all of a sudden, my healthy choice was coming back to haunt me because I just was not prepared... By Sunday I am really worried – the zit was a red – rimmed volcano, huge and definitely a problem under my bra strap. Monday, I go to see the Doctor.

I'm so bummed out that I hear little of what the doctor is talking about, but I hear "infection" and "take pills". Then I lean in when I hear "Epsom salts" and "apply hot compress four times a day for ten minutes". Ok, I buy the pills and the huge bag of Epsom salts. Luckily, I can get a store clerk to help me drag this huge bag of salt to the car. I happily start taking the pills and applying the Epsom salts four times a day. Soon the zit blows – good news – it was the middle of the night with minimum loss of life! The Epsom salts did their job drawing out the poison. I soon HATE the Epsom salt routine. I'm applying salt to an open wound. Isn't there a saying about this? This salt application is HARD; I now know why I didn't choose the "sickness". I suffer four times a day ten minutes each time! That's forty minutes of suffering a day! I did the math!

Finally, I go back to the clinic. Sorry, my doctor is not available and it will take many hours to see the one other harried doctor on that night. I ask the so-called nurse on the desk about my wound. She is reluctant to go out on a limb and actually tell me what to do. She gives me a web site! A web site?

So... I go see a pharmacist. SHE is willing to go out on a limb and say, no, you don't need any more salt....

But I worry – what will I do with the hole, will it ever heal, will all that pus continue to drain forever? Will I get more bad zits; am I now prone to these; will it eventually turn into cancer? And, what will I do with that huge bag of Epsom salts if I don't get any more large and gross zits? Should I carry the salt in the car for traction in the winter?

Hey, now that's a good idea!

This "historic site" is now a blackhead. Not often squeezed due to the angle, but still a source of amusement...

Summertime Blues

Tune: Summertime

Summertime... is it here? Is it over?
What a bummer
Besides the mosquitoes; I have to shave...
My legs
Little black hairs
Get out the lawn mower
My sex life ain't no screamin' Hell either

Then I met this guy
You know the one,
Likes to drive by real fast and roll down his window
Likes to share his loud music
And his tattoo
OOO OOO
But you know what?
He didn't like my hairy legs either
So that's why I'm singing
The Summertime Blues!

I needed to put all the annoying things in my life into a song. It was very heartfelt at the time...

Susan Carter

The Fascist Cat Bylaw

Fort Saskatchewan, Alberta

January 2, 1992

Dear Nancy White and friends at Sunday Morning

I really enjoyed your Sunday morning Cabaret and I would like to nominate nine people to your "Hall of Losers" ...

In Fort Saskatchewan, as of yesterday, there is a CAT BYLAW in place. I am nominating first of all the five people who have complained about felines in our city, and second of all the four town counsellors who voted it in!

Five people who have changed the lives of 12,500 souls in Fort Saskatchewan surely deserve some credit. There are 12,500 people in Fort Saskatchewan, and I'm not sure how many cats. But these five annoy – mouse people can now take credit for causing neighbors to "turn in" furry friends and causing children's pets to disappear into the bowels of the city – forever – because daddy won't pay the fine – on principle.

The four counsellors who bowed to five lobbying cat-haters surely deserve a special place in the Hall of Losers. I have heard rumors that a child died eating a cat bowel movement in a sand box. What an epidemic, I'm sure I will lie in bed at night and worry about my child in sandboxes. Yes, I can see why four counsellors decided to "end" the cats' bowel movements! I can see where this will be an issue in our federal government – surely when we are deciding the fate of Canada, the fate of our felines should be decided upon as well, yes perhaps the United Nations should worry about cats as well as the starving people. I have had Christmas tree lights stolen this year, and I know some clever cat is at the bottom of this horrible crime – I'm positive that all teenagers are kept on leashes at night, and surely, they could not be responsible for this awful deed.

I for one want to go on record as definitely approving of the thousands of tax dollars that are necessarily spent to keep these horrible defecating thieving creatures OUT of my yard. At least two people will have jobs running around trapping cats, processing and paw-printing and this will make the Federal Government spend more money on a study to expand the programme to the whole country!

Thank you

P.S. If our furry teenaged son, Killer Cat comes visiting your yard, please call me, I'd be very happy to drag him home and lecture him about the dangers of running around town... unprotected!

City of Fort Saskatchewan
Animal Control Bylaw
Bylaw No. C7-16
Here are a few of the 20 Sections
With Fun Facts...
Fines up to $1000

2. DEFINITIONS

b. "At Large" shall mean and includes the situation where: i. a dog, nuisance dog, restricted dog, or cat is found on any place other than the owner's property

c. "Cat" shall mean either a male or female of the felidae family

3.6 Licences issued under this Bylaw shall not be transferrable between a dog, nuisance dog, restricted dog, or cat.

4.8 The owner of a dog, nuisance dog, restricted dog, or cat shall not permit the animal to:

a. threaten or bite a person; Bylaw C7-16 Page 5 City of Fort Saskatchewan Animal Control Bylaw C7-16 Office Consolidation 2017
b. chase a motor vehicle;

c. chase a person

d. bark, howl, or meow.

5. DEFECATION

5.1 The owner of a dog, nuisance dog, restricted dog, or cat shall remove any defecation left by the animal on public or private property, other than the owner's property

6. NOISE

6.1 The owner of a dog, nuisance dog, restricted dog, or cat shall not permit the animal to bark, howl, or meow excessively.

11. SEIZURE AND IMPOUNDING

11.1 A Peace Officer is authorized to seize and impound any animal found contrary to any provision in this Bylaw.

A word about drugs...

So, I quit smoking in grade 3. True. I started in January, 1960 when we moved to Wadena, Saskatchewan I was in the middle of grade one. The new neighborhood consisted of a number of teen-agers who were smoking. One of the teen-agers became my babysitter. We would all go to the outhouse to smoke whatever cigarettes were available. I became the cute kid who bought the cigarettes. In those days, I just said I was buying them for my mom. At that time my mom smoked, so it was a believable lie. I got no pleasure from the smoking, just a guilty feeling buying cigarettes – that were not for Mom. When the family moved to another teen-ager-free neighborhood, I quit smoking!

I did inhale Marijuana. It was at movie night when I was in university. Wow, it was pretty strong; I remember the headache. I didn't get any pleasure or euphoria from the Marijuana, just a headache. I did a drug for a "condition". I felt like I was in a deep dark visceral stream trying to swim against the current. I felt my brain take a second longer than normal to understand instructions. I quit the drug. I'm too close to death to become addicted at my age.

I tried taking pain killers. That Oxycontin just made me weep. I wasn't weeping about the second break to my kneecap, I was just weeping. The drug didn't cure my pain, so after seriously thinking about selling the pills at a local junior high, I took them back to the pharmacy. Ice. Numbing the pain kept me sane, the weeping pills didn't do the job. Is ice a drug, perhaps? I know for sure that it's a re-cycled drug. Just refreeze that blue jell and hey, more drug. I can see that if I get to "junky stage" that you'd need more and more bags of ice to get the high, but, it's an idea.

I have hung on to two drugs, just to re-assure myself that I'm NOT dead. My old age pension keeps me in coffee and chocolate! At the time of writing this, I'm now getting over $21.00 a day from the government of Canada – I'm still amazed that someone is giving me money for just being me...

Mouse Murder Mysteries

2006

Dedicated to Orion – cat number three –
in loving memory

It's my daughter's fault... really. She was NOT thinking of her inheritance when she needed a home for her cat because her new place didn't take pets. Convenient. We now have a cute, red, male, mostly finished growing cat. I felt sorry for the cat because of the size of our patio that is a ten-by-ten square of concrete surrounded by an eight-foot wooden fence. I provide the cat with a cat door fitted into a window so he can use the patio at night. A few insects coming inside could be dealt with to provide our new family member with some fresh air.

We soon find out that the cat is a great hunter – not a killer, just a hunter. He brings a mouse into the house to play with. We hear the scrabbling of mouse and cat. I'm puzzled, how does a cat catch a mouse on the ten-by-ten cement patio that is pretending to be a yard? All those nature shows I've watched have not explained this cat's M.O. How does he lure it into his clutches; does he crook his cat nail and say, "Here Mousy, Mousy"? Does the cat advertise on those internet dating services? Marital status wouldn't be important, in fact the sexual leaning wouldn't matter either. Nationality of the mouse would have no importance, but perhaps the cat would advertise that a rodent into S and M would be a bonus. Whatever his cat technique is, the little man does his job and helps the mouse to that big field in the sky. I won't go into details, but it involves a lot of cursing, rustling and a fly swatter. The cursing would be at me who has watched too many old movies on T.V. The movies show the female on the furniture screaming. I follow this model by staying ON the bed. Instead of screaming, I repeatedly ask, "But what can I do"?

Mouse number two is found expired in the basement. Due to my forensic knowledge (again from T.V.); I have deduced cause of death was a heart attack. No autopsy was performed.

Mouse number three is in the house two nights before the little man moves furniture and inadvertently and unintentionally squashes the mouse under the filing cabinet. You may wonder how we knew there was a third visitor. Examining the demeanor of the cat made us realize there was something.... the cat's ears were ever in listening mode. While in the bathroom, the cat would be listening to the closed cupboard doors. It was very freaky. The three of us that were still living, cat, the little man and I, continue to look for the mouse. Soon the cat's ears have gone back to normal and I carry on with my regular activities. I'm filing some bills and notice a noxious smell. The humans hoist the filing cabinet and remove the two-dimensional corpse as the cat catches up on his sleep. It has been exhausting for him – up all night looking for his playmate definitely took a toll on the feline family member.

After a few days of calm, I feel I can safely remove the evidence of mouse occupation because I think that the mice have figured out the cat's hunting techniques and have removed themselves from danger. Sucking mouse droppings up with the vacuum that is long past it's prime is not easy. I'm on my hands and knees cursing the short hose and even shorter nozzle of my long-past-warranty vacuum.

I didn't realize that I'd done such a thorough job of cleaning what is apparently a top-rated B. and B. for mice. Mouse number four is in the house luxuriating in the clean mouse guest room for five days. You-know-who's ears have again given us the clues needed to decide that we had another guest. For most of the five days I'm working on my very first question.... how does he lure them? Did the advertisement read, "Lonely male (fixed) seeking companionship"? Could this mouse be a pregnant female, searching for a father figure for her offspring? I'm horrified by this thought and not about the father figure idea... I try to work at home, but visions of a future little mouse community keep flowing through my work. One evening I see the mouse running for a food cupboard upstairs. I'm shocked and I don't know what to do. I thought mice would just stay downstairs where the cat took them. The little man is very informative telling me that this mouse is a climber. He figured that out when the mouse was looking down on him from the shower curtain rod while he (the little man not the cat) was naked and wet.

Perhaps we're feeding the cat too well. He catches number four each night but takes it to the bathroom to have his way with it. The little man recruits me as his lackey, and then demands help building barriers – all at two in the morning. We have the elusive mouse cornered at one point by herding him through a narrow channel in the barricade. Unfortunately, I did not do my job well. I realize that building a barricade with an ironing board and flimsy rotary cutting board leaves a lot to be desired in the engineering department of our marriage. I also fail in the liberated woman oath I took. Visions of number four running over my bare feet freaks me shrieking out.

As the clock ticks closer to morning, we build another barricade. You may wonder where the cat was... he retired the field after he was turned off by the whapping flyswatter during the first herding/annihilation attempt by the little man. We discuss our plan of attack. We have our backs to the door since we have now learned that the little devil can scoot quickly under mere doors. We are reluctant warriors cursing, rustling and swatting. With one lucky swat, we claim temporary victory.

I call it temporary victory because I am now consumed with fear of doing this again. What will I do when the cat decides to bring in number five and the little man is away on business? Will that peanut butter in the live trap actually work this time? Or will I have to use major fire power; an Uzi or a 747: Wait... is one of those an airplane? Should I retire the cat door: What will the cat do for entertainment? Place another ad? Should I search for a new vacuum: What will I do with a full night's sleep? AND... Why the bathroom?

Epilogue

Some weeks later a friend told us about her friends that occupied another unit in our four-plex; they had mouse problems too. The friends had successfully used a trap. Ah... mouse number five eluded the cat by going to what he/she thought was neutral territory. Our mouse problems were resolved... well, for a while...

Time Line
In case you're confused...

1925   Ida Mae Selena Coulthard born in Dunrae, Manitoba – October 16

1928   Vernon Ralph Robinson born in Estevan, Saskatchewan – October 16

1949   Alan born in Wingham, Ontario

1953   Susan born in Weyburn, Saskatchewan

1960   The Robinsons, Vern, Mae, Susan and Don move to Wadena, Saskatchewan

1968   Susan starts teaching swim lessons

1970   Susan attends University in Regina, Saskatchewan taking Education

1973   Susan and Alan meet on a blind date in Collingwood, Ontario

1974   Married... after Susan graduates – living in Southern Ontario
       Lived in London, Simcoe, Blenheim and Stratford (five places)

	Susan is subbing, Alan works in banks - they kept changing names
1980	Moved to Edmonton, Alberta, Susan keeps subbing
	Lived in two places
1981	Full time teaching Junior High School in Fort Saskatchewan, Alberta
1983	Kristel born in Edmonton, Alberta
1986	The three of us, plus cat, move to Fort Saskatchewan
	Lived in seven places
1993	Started doing Stand up – training as an amateur at Yuk Yuks and with church groups in Fort Saskatchewan
1995	Won third place as a stand up in Edmonton's Pride in Edmonton. Sixty contestants.
2009	Retired to Nova Scotia. Kingston, Aylesford and Berwick.
	Had three places; lived in two. Always looking for new friends.

But Susan immediately breaks her kneecap (took two years to heal). So, she wrote a book about teaching art.

Susan, when she hasn't got a broken bone of some sort, continues to sub and do stand up. Working in a Fabric Store was fun for five years... spending the pay cheque on fabric kept her in "projects" for the whole pandemic...

| 2019 | We decide to move back to Alberta to be closer to family. AND of course, to hunker down in a new place with absolutely no friends. So, I worked on this book... |
| | Only lived in one place here, so far. If you're counting our married abodes, it should add up to eighteen! |

Thank you

To my family who have helped me along the way...

Mom and Dad for supporting my crazy idea to do stand up. Dad for encouraging me to be funny. I was an adult before I realized that when I was growing up, females weren't supposed to be funny.

Alan for helping me get determined by telling me that doing stand up was a stupid idea. He changed his mind when I got paid the first time!

My daughter for teaching me that kids don't always respond to the rah-rah cry of "just try it". She tried "it" when she was ready.

And while I'm waxing on about family – Thank you to my favourite son-in-law for helping with all my renos, and being so good to Kristel

Aaron and Braden; you are just a joy, Thank you...

To my illustrators; Susanne Ritchie and David Shkolny (David is a former student!)

To my Nova Scotia "friend from away" Erica who read every story and told me what didn't make sense

AND, thank YOU for making it to the end of the book....

If you like the book, send me a line at sccomic@live.com

If you don't like the book, just drop it off at your local Senior Centre!

Story index

Susan Carter at Pagemaster
https://pagemasterpublishing.ca/by/susan-carter/

To order more copies of this book, find books by other Canadian authors, or make inquiries about publishing your own book, contact PageMaster at:

PageMaster Publication Services Inc.
11340-120 Street, Edmonton, AB T5G 0W5
books@pagemaster.ca
780-425-9303

catalogue and e-commerce store
PageMasterPublishing.ca/Shop

About the Author

As a speaker, teacher and comic, Susan Carter always found humour in everyday situations. She thought she had a nice life until she became a senior! If comedy comes from pain, Susan is experiencing lots of comedy from the many annoyances that have come with her "advancing" years. She performs and writes to relieve the stress of others who are also "counting their years"!